The
Wall

Rebuilding a culture of *life* in America—
and ending abortion as we know it

To Nanci,

[signature]

Col. 4:17
5/4/17

By Kirk Walden

Published by LifeTrends ♦ Nashville, Tennessee

To order copies of *The Wall*, visit www.wallofhopechallenge.com.
Visit Kirk Walden on the web at www.kirkwalden.com.

All Scripture Quotations, unless otherwise noted, are taken from:
The New American Standard Bible (NASB)
Scripture taken from the NEW AMERICAN STANDARD BIBLE®,
Copyright © 1960,1962,1963,1968,1971,1972,1973,1975,1977,1995
by The Lockman Foundation. Used by permission.

Copyright ©2013 Kirk Walden
Published by LifeTrends, Goodlettsville, TN
Printed in the United States of America

ISBN 978-0-9896399-1-0

The Wall is dedicated to Jennifer . . .

A wonderful wife, an amazing mother, my best friend,
and my teammate forever.

-The Wall-

Contents

Chapter 1
A Time for New Hope

If you consider yourself pro-life; if you believe in protecting the most innocent and vulnerable among us, you may be somewhat weary by now. After 40 years of Roe v. Wade and more than one million lives lost to abortion each year, I understand the frustration and the fatigue.

And if we look to Washington for change, the news is hardly encouraging. The current occupant of the White House passionately defends the Roe decision, appoints to key posts only those who join him in celebrating abortion, and makes Planned Parenthood a key component of his speaking schedule (and his budget). If this isn't enough, his health care plan steamrolls those with a pro-life conscience while bowing down at the altar of the abortion industry.

So when you read the following paragraph, you might be skeptical. I understand. Because what you are about to read, in light of the current United States social and political climate, is seemingly far-fetched. But here is what I believe:

Right now, we have an opportunity to give rise to an incredible endeavor that could drop America's abortion rate by 75% or more, to pre-1973 levels. If, at this moment in history, we choose to roll up our sleeves and take a few practical and effective steps, *in the next decade* we can see unprecedented results that will usher in victory after victory and ultimately, create a new generation where life is celebrated and honored once again.

Impossible? Many will say so. But it can be done.

If we choose to take the simple route proposed in these pages, it is possible to approach the point of ending *the thought* of abortion in our country. The result of this could even spawn a spiritual revival unlike anything we've seen in our lifetimes and perhaps for generations.

Really? Yes.

Here is even more encouragement: these steps, and the resulting victories we will see, will not depend on a particular candidate or election, on a court decision or on some brand-new gimmick or program. In fact, should we as Christians choose to build on a foundation God has already put in place for us, our efforts will initiate a seismic shift that will usher in a new culture of life in America.

After 40 years of legalized abortion across the country, I understand why many would question my thinking. But I promise you, I'm not crazy.

In fact, I've got a bit of experience in the pro-life realm; 33 years of it. For the last 22 of those years, my full-time mission has been to advance life-affirming organizations all over the country. More on that later, but for now, know this: ten years ago I would not have believed this endeavor possible. Even five years ago I would have questioned it. But today, I'm confident: we can achieve a virtually abortion-free America.

This book is a simple, brief outline of the path to creating this new culture of life in America. This will be a culture built not on elections, judicial decisions or even the court of public opinion. Instead, we will change our society by raising a powerful Wall of Hope, built by you and me, with God's favor as our strength.

In the following pages I want to take you on a journey to 2500 sites where this Wall is quietly rising, America's pregnancy help centers (PHCs). Some of these centers, perhaps a few dozen, have been with us since before Roe; a couple of hundred more came on the scene in the late 70s. In the 80s and 90s, the number boomed to nearly 2000. Today, you might be surprised at what these 2500+ centers are accomplishing behind the scenes.

From time to time you may hear of your local pregnancy help center through your church. You might contribute financially to its work; you may even volunteer in some capacity. Even if you are familiar with PHCs, you may not yet realize that these centers can be the key to ending America's culture of abortion and turning our society back toward life once again. Give me a few minutes of your time however, and I believe you will.

The truth is, even now some of these centers are altering the cultural landscape around them. I can tell you of a pregnancy help center in the South that is a key player in lowering its county's abortion rate by 55% in the last 12 years. It's a stunning figure, and this center is only warming up. In the next seven years they expect to take on the final 45%, and win.

Though pregnancy help centers have been in the process of building this Wall of Hope for quite some time, it is *now* when their impact is about to become more powerful than ever. The pieces are now in place for effective growth; the result of that growth being a stunning, surprising and joyful downturn in America's abortion rate, possibly back to pre-Roe v. Wade levels.

Pre Roe levels? Yes. And perhaps, we will see the day when abortion is virtually obsolete in our country. Really. This means hundreds of abortion centers closing their doors, as one in Ohio did recently, due to "lack of patient volume."

In the process, we will see babies born so that they can

experience their first smiles, their first steps and their first birthdays. We will see fathers step forward as never before to join in raising their sons and daughters. We will see many single-parent families become joyful, two-parent families. And we will see many of those who choose life make a simple decision that will change their futures: They will choose to follow Jesus Christ.

In addition, we will see something more. Those who have experienced an abortion in their past will find forgiveness, healing and hope. For the first time, they will be free from a decision that has haunted them for months, years or decades.

When we soon complete this Wall of Hope, the Roe decision, now with us for an entire generation, will not suddenly disappear. But its grip on us will weaken. Its impact will diminish and regardless of how long its words stay with us, its stronghold will be replaced by a new power: Life, energized by the Body of Christ.

If you are discouraged by the decline we see in our society today, and troubled by the loss of life and the pain so many are struggling with as a result of a past abortion decision, today is the day to take heart. We are about to build a Wall of Hope; and this Wall is about to usher in a new generation: A generation of *Life*.

Somewhere on this Wall, you will discover the perfect location where you can join in this compelling endeavor. And when you find your place on The Wall of Hope, I think you will say to yourself, "Now *that* is something I can do." As we join in building this Wall, together we will accomplish what seems impossible: our culture will turn away from abortion in record numbers, toward life.

Before we look at the future however, I need you to join me for a trip back in history, about 2400 years or so. Here, we can look into the life of another who saw a challenge and vowed to conquer it through the building of a Wall of Hope.

You know Nehemiah from the Old Testament. He's the Wall builder who took on an impossible task and completed his mission in just 52 days. If we delve into his life, I think we will find the keys to building *our* Wall of Hope. Our Wall is already starting to rise. In the coming decade, I believe we will bring it to completion.

Through Nehemiah, let's find out how.

-The Wall-

Chapter 2
A Hero's Entrance onto an Unlikely Stage

In the movies, the hero rarely shows up exactly when expected. Instead, the star's "saving the day moment" always takes place much later than we can imagine, at a time when all hope seems lost. This dynamic takes place in Scripture too, in the riveting story of Nehemiah.

As we read the Book of Nehemiah, we'll find that he, and those he led, rebuilt the Wall of Jerusalem in just 52 days; an amazing story of leadership, courage and determination. But before Nehemiah placed his first brick in the wall, so much time went by that one might have wondered if there was any hope at all left for him and the Jewish people.

Nehemiah's work began in 445 BC, but the story of the Wall of Jerusalem begins 160 years earlier, in 605 BC with the first siege of Jerusalem, starting what we know as The Babylonian Captivity. At that time, Daniel and other Israelites were enslaved by Babylonian King Nebuchadnezzar. Two other attacks upon Jerusalem took place later; one around 597 BC (when Ezekiel was taken captive). So far, the wall was still standing.

Ten years later however, Nebuchadnezzar roared into Jerusalem again. During this final siege he broke through the Wall. The Babylonian King burned the gates of the city, reduced the Wall of Jerusalem to rubble in many places, and killed the sons of King Zedekiah of Judah. Finally, he blinded Zedekiah, shackled him and forced him into captivity. Many other leading citizens of Judah were put to death. The Wall of Jerusalem was in ruins by 586 BC, more than 140 years before Nehemiah's project began.

For the Jewish people, The Babylonian Captivity was one of their most painful chapters. And while it would be nice to say that their captivity ended with a glorious Jewish uprising, it didn't. Instead, the Jews found freedom through an outsider, King Cyrus of Persia. Cyrus overthrew Babylon around 538 B.C. and upon taking power, granted the Jews permission to return to Jerusalem. In addition, Cyrus' decree urged the people to rebuild their altars and temples; and resume worship of their God.

And return they did. Within two years, nearly 50,000 Jewish settlers journeyed back to Jerusalem to rebuild. All seemed well and the motivation to return Jerusalem to its former glory appeared to gather momentum. The altar was restored in just months, in time for the Feast of Booths.

But the work on the temple, begun with shouts of praise and thanksgiving, halted within a year because of fear and discouragement. Years of political struggle ensued while rebuilding ceased.

Pause with me a moment here, because this book is not about Nehemiah, but about us. My goal is to give all of us a plan to build our modern day Wall of Hope, a Wall that will protect women and men from being exploited and victimized by abortion, and a Wall that will save the lives of literally millions of children.

But before we can complete our wall, we've got to recognize that we too, have been stifled in many ways. We've been discouraged, ridiculed, shouted down and vilified. And if we want to throw our political battles into the mix, let's be honest and say that while we are seeing some victories, overall we've had a rough go of things.

For the Jews of that day, the discouragement, fear and political battles were constant struggles. The prophets Haggai and Zechariah led the people to complete work on the Temple in 516 (more than 20 years after the return) but the Wall of Jerusalem continued to lie in ruins, leaving all of Jerusalem vulnerable. Nothing would change until Nehemiah came on the scene in 445 BC, a whopping *93 years* following the return to Jerusalem.

The timeline here is important because if you are like me, we read the Bible and turn the pages without sometimes realizing how many years are passing throughout the chapters in front of us. Until recently, I had not bothered to do the math on Nehemiah's story.

Ninety-three years is a long, long time. For us, going back 93 years means heading to 1920 and 1921. Warren Harding was elected President in 1920; Babe Ruth was sold by the Red Sox to the Yankees in 1920. In that same year, a fellow named Walter Elias Disney took his first job as an artist, for $40 a week with KC Slide Company. And in 1920, The American Pro Football association was founded (now the NFL), and the 18th Amendment, giving us prohibition, went into effect..

In 1921 the Yankees, with Ruth on the roster, purchased 20 acres in the Bronx for a new home known as Yankee Stadium. Americans heard the first radio broadcast of a sporting event, a boxing match; and also heard its first religious broadcast, via KDKA in Pittsburgh. Albert Einstein gave a lecture on a new theory known as "Relativity." And in 1921, Franklin Delano Roosevelt, who would later serve nearly four full terms as our president, was struck with polio.

Since those days, the United States has sworn in 16 more presidents and "The House that Ruth Built," Yankee Stadium, is no more. Mr. Disney moved on from his first job to a Mickey Mouse occupation, which paid him well. We've repealed the 18th Amendment (with the 21st Amendment) and added several more Amendments as well; one of them giving women the right to vote. And from its modest beginnings, the former American Pro Football Association's signature event, The Super Bowl, is one of our country's most-watched events, every year. As for the disease that burdened FDR, the United States has not seen a polio case in more than 40 years.

For us then, the last 90-plus years have brought plenty of change. But for the Jews, ninety-three years passed without one person stepping forward to rebuild the wall. Not one.

Here is a fascinating question for all of us to consider when we think of Nehemiah's story: Why didn't God move earlier, so that the wall could be rebuilt? Why couldn't God have touched the heart of some other hero, at an earlier time?

We don't know, of course. But what if God *did* move earlier? What if, at points during those 93 years, God called upon others to perform a mighty deed and rebuild the wall, and the answer was "No"?

We don't know if that happened. But if someone said "no" to God, it wasn't the first time. Remember the story of the spies in chapters 13 and 14 of the Book of Numbers? You know what happened: Moses sent 12 spies, one from each tribe of Israel, to scout out the Land of Canaan, a territory God promised to give to the Sons of Israel.

Of the 12, Joshua and Caleb reported the land to be bountiful and the two were confident in conquering the inhabitants. The other ten spies however, saw the same set of facts and said "No." As a result, the new nation that would be Israel had to wait another 40 years before entering the Promised Land.

When we consider the wall of Jerusalem, in ruins during those 90-plus years between Cyrus' decree and Nehemiah, we can guess that there were plenty of defeatists in the city. These naysayers probably looked at the crumbling wall in front of them and said, "This is too large a task and there are too few people to complete the work. We can never make this wall strong enough to stop our enemies."

I point this out because there are those who might read this book and say, "This country is going down the tubes, the culture is getting worse and the best we can do is to slow the inevitable decline." In other words, the "giants in our land" are too many and too large to overcome.

With respect, I disagree. I believe that instead of decrying the current state of our culture, we need to be changing our culture. And when it comes to protecting the sanctity of life, we need those who will say "Yes" to God and join in building our Wall of Hope.

Yes, Roe has been with us for an entire generation, 40 years. But as we respond to the call to build our Wall, we will loosen its hold on our society. We don't have to wait another 40 years or another 40 days. In a few pages we'll see our plan to build unfold and we can begin taking action, action that can forever change the direction of a nation.

Getting back to our example from the Book of Numbers, Joshua and Caleb said, "Yes." And while a generation died out for saying "no," God allowed those two to enter the Promised Land. And Nehemiah? Faced with an incredible task, he said "Yes" as well.

Nehemiah had no resources at his disposal. He did not know whether anyone would join him. But he didn't waver. A job had to be done, and he made the choice to step forward. Nehemiah's is a story of an ordinary man who trusted in an extraordinary God.

We can, too.

Chapter 3
Crushing News
(Nehemiah 1:1-4)

The taste of the king's drink lingered on his lips as Nehemiah stood outside, in the main portico of King Artaxerxes' palace. He touched his finger to his lips and wiped away the last vestiges of his day's work. As cupbearer to the king, sampling food and drink was routine. Nehemiah had almost reached the point where this portion of his role in the palace was mundane.

Still, every day was a new day and each morning the nagging thought would slip into his consciousness: *Would this be the day?* Would his next sip, or his next bite, be the beginning of his last moments on this Earth?

Today was not going to be that day; Nehemiah knew that now. More than an hour had passed and there were no repercussions from his inspection of the king's delicacies. Now, Nehemiah was alone with his thoughts, waiting for word from his brother, Hanani.

Nehemiah gazed at the sky, running his fingers through his salt-and-pepper beard as the sun dropped beyond the horizon. He was nervous, and he couldn't escape it.

A burden regarding the wall of Jerusalem had been on Nehemiah's mind for months. Was it the Lord God who was piercing his thoughts? He did not know for certain.

From a common sense standpoint, the Wall of Jerusalem was none of Nehemiah's concern. He lived in Artaxerxes' palace, far away from his brothers, the Israelites. If they didn't care about their wall of protection, why should he? Yet the gnawing idea that his people were unprotected was becoming almost impossible to bear.

That's why he had sent his brother, Hanani, to gather information on the status of the wall. *Surely Jerusalem is safe tonight,* he hoped. But he was far from sure.

Instead of pondering the condition of the wall, Nehemiah tried to think of other things. He reminded himself of the life he had, a life that had its dangers of course, but also its benefits. As cupbearer he was often called upon by King Artaxerxes for counsel. *Adonai has given you the King's ear,* he told himself. *Your words have saved hundreds of your brothers. You live in a palace!*

Nehemiah shook his head, knowing he could never convince himself that everything was okay; not until he knew of Jerusalem's condition. Not until he could lay his head down knowing, without doubt, that the Children of Israel too, were sleeping in safety. Hanani would give him good news. Surely, he would.

If his calculations were correct, Hanani would come today, sometime during the evening. A chill rushed through Nehemiah's body. Perhaps, he reasoned, this was a sign from the Lord that news was close.

Nehemiah looked down, nudging a loose pebble with his sandal. He pulled his cloak around his neck, noticing the walkway's bricks becoming darker as the last vestiges of sunlight began to disappear. Maybe he would have to wait another day. "I will not sleep then," he said aloud to no one.

His declaration was simple, sincere. Nehemiah was not angry. But deep in his heart he knew the time of reckoning was upon him. If the Lord God would not send an answer now, Nehemiah knew he would not be able to rest until the answer came.

He had to know.

Moment of truth

A clearing throat behind him interrupted Nehemiah's thoughts. "Your brother," another of the servants declared quietly. "He—and others from Judah. They are here."

Nehemiah's station was one of the highest in the King's quarters; the servant's approach was one of deference. Nehemiah nodded, accepting the interruption. "Send them out to me."

"As you wish," the servant answered, taking his leave.

Nehemiah breathed a long sigh. He would know in minutes.

He heard the rustling of their steps before they entered the portico. Their voices were hushed. *Not a good sign*, Nehemiah thought.

Hanani entered first, reaching out for an embrace. Nehemiah accepted his brother's kiss and gave his own. Hanani held his grip on his brother's shoulders longer than Nehemiah expected, as if he were about to tell of the loss of a loved one. A sense of foreboding enveloped Nehemiah. Tension rose in his arms. He felt a quiver in his hand.

Introductions were made. There were no smiles. All knew what Nehemiah was about to ask.

Nehemiah could tell by looking in the eyes of his guests that the news would not be good. Each man looked tired, withdrawn. They looked him in the eye only briefly before glancing elsewhere. Two looked down, unable to meet Nehemiah's gaze at all.

Nehemiah took a deep breath, dreading the response even before his inquiry.

"Tell me of Jerusalem," Nehemiah said. "How are those who returned? Are they well? Are they rebuilding? And the wall; does it stand strong?"

Nehemiah studied the faces of Hanani and the others. None

wanted to break the silence. Finally, one by one they spoke, dropping the truth like a hammer. One sentence stuck with him more than any other: "The remnant there in the province who survived the captivity is in great distress and reproach, and the wall of Jerusalem is broken down. Its gates are burned with fire."

There. Now he knew. No more questions, no more wondering. Perhaps the news could have been worse, but Nehemiah could not imagine how. He turned from the men and looked outward toward the sunset, allowing a tear to slip down his cheek. *The walls are just as Nebuchadnezzar left them,* he thought to himself. *Nothing's been done. As soon as an enemy approaches, they will be finished. The men, the women, the children. All will be gone. Again.*

Within minutes Hanani and the others from Judah left Nehemiah alone with his thoughts. *"The walls of Jerusalem are broken down."* Those words somehow hurt the most. Broken down walls, Nehemiah knew, meant a broken people within those walls.

For them, every day and every night was wrought with fear and desperation. The people were defenseless and without hope, dreading the moment when they would be overtaken and enslaved. Or killed.

Nehemiah wept. And Nehemiah prayed.

Deep down Nehemiah knew that soon, he would take action. He was going to Jerusalem. And he was going to rebuild that wall, no matter what.

Nehemiah's first key to our Wall of Hope: Desire

Nehemiah knew that without the protection of the wall, his people were vulnerable and plagued with fear. Nehemiah understood the history of his people, and knew where fear would lead. Just after

22

crossing the Red Sea, the Israelites begged Moses to take them back to Egypt. Why? Fear over lack of resources.

We just mentioned the story of the twelve spies and the Land of Canaan. Why didn't the Israelites immediately go in and take the land? Fear. Of supposed giants in the land.

Fear usually results in poor decisions. Nehemiah grasped this truth, and we do, too.

When we consider the mothers and fathers who are facing crisis pregnancies, we know they are often controlled by fear of the unknown. This leads to vulnerability. The truth is that few go to abortion centers because they think this option is a great idea; they go because they are scared and afraid.

Those dealing with fear, whether the Israelites of Nehemiah's day or those in crisis situations today, need hope. Nehemiah saw that a rebuilt Wall of Jerusalem would provide not only protection, but hope and courage, too.

Interestingly, the Book of Nehemiah does not show us a watershed moment where God speaks directly to Nehemiah and says, "Rebuild the Wall of Jerusalem." There is no burning bush, no voice coming out of the heavens.

What we do see however, is a man with a God-given desire to save his people. This desire ultimately led to Nehemiah's taking decisive action.

Because you are reading this book, I'm taking an educated guess that you have a desire; a God-given desire just like Nehemiah, to reach out to those who are fearful and give them hope. In the case of the Jewish people, that hope began to build as the Wall of Jerusalem rose.

We can build our Wall of Hope, a 21st century version of

Nehemiah's wall, and we can reach those who are fearful with tremendous, life-giving alternatives to the abortion centers across the country. If we do this, they will run inside our Wall of Hope instead of making decisions based on fear.

We start then, with Desire. From there, Nehemiah asked God to give him success. We can do the same.

This leads us to the second key.

Chapter 4
An Audience with the King
(Nehemiah 1:4—2:8)

Nehemiah took a deep breath and placed his fingers around the glass of wine as he took a cautious step in the direction of the King's quarters. For four months now, ever since receiving the crushing news from his brother, he had taken great care to perform his duties without revealing his inner struggle.

Yet every day while going about his work, another mission; of a wall that had to be rebuilt, overwhelmed him.

In front of King Artaxerxes, Nehemiah determined to always hold his head high. But in every private moment he could find, Nehemiah prayed to the Lord on behalf of his people, asking God for an opportunity to go to Jerusalem.

In the last few days, those prayers had become even more urgent, more focused, more powerful. Nehemiah realized he was no longer simply praying; he was in fact, crying out for God's blessing on his dream to rebuild the wall.

But even with all of his prayers, Nehemiah struggled with a sense of fear. As much as he wanted to take on the impossible, a roadblock stood in his path. A cupbearer did not simply resign to take on a new opportunity. And few kings were willing to let such a trusted confidant stroll out the door to try his hand at another project in a far-off land.

If given a chance to speak to the king, Nehemiah wondered if he would be convincing at all. Perhaps he would simply blurt out a string of nonsensical pleas and Artaxerxes would whisk him away with a dismissive wave of his hand. Nehemiah didn't know about that. All he understood was that he would have to try.

Earlier in the day, the prayers rushed out of him as he lifted his arms toward heaven: "We have acted very corruptly against You and have not kept the commandments, nor the statutes, nor the ordinances which You commanded Your servant Moses!" He exclaimed. The pain of knowing how *his* people, the very ones who *knew* the living God, had betrayed Him, was almost too much to bear.

And yet, Nehemiah knew God had not forgotten His people. "Remember the word which You commanded Your servant Moses when you said, 'If you are unfaithful I will scatter you among the peoples; *but* if you return to Me and keep My commandments and do them, though those of you who have been scattered were in the most remote part of the heavens, I will gather them from there and will bring them to the place where I have chosen to cause My name to dwell.'"

Nehemiah clenched his fists as his voice rose. Whether it was raw emotion, or a spiritual revival in his soul, Nehemiah wasn't sure. All he knew was that he was going to pray until he got an answer. The strength in him was growing, and somewhere inside he knew that yes, the Lord God would respond, somehow. And now, with a renewed sense of purpose, he spoke more boldly before his God.

"And they are Your servants, and Your people whom You redeemed by *Your* great power and by *Your* strong hand . . ."

As soon as he spoke those words, something clicked in Nehemiah. If someone were to ask him about it, Nehemiah could not have explained the sense of expectancy that engulfed him. But at that moment, after declaring the power of the living God,

Nehemiah was confident that somewhere in the heavens, a Hand was moving to reach out, to touch a people and perform a work that Nehemiah could not yet imagine.

Nehemiah drew a breath, and with a passion he had never before experienced, a voice he did not recognize as his own burst forth from deep within his soul: "O Lord, I *beg* of You, may Your ear be attentive to the prayer of Your servant and the prayer of Your servants who delight to revere your name, and make Your servant successful today, and grant him compassion before this man."

Once those words left his lips, Nehemiah fell to his knees. Tears poured down his cheeks. Nothing more needed to be said. His answer was near, he knew that now.

So as he stood outside Artaxerxes' door, a door fashioned from the impressive timber of Asaph's forest, Nehemiah realized that this night could be the culmination of those prayers, one way or the other. A quickening in his spirit told him a prayer was about to be answered. His moment was in front of him.

Nehemiah thought of his forefathers, those who had shown exceptional faith and courage. He considered Abraham, who left everything to follow his God. And Moses, who dared to stand before Pharaoh. And David, who slew the Philistine giant. Would his courage be the same?

Nehemiah cleared his throat, unsure as to whether he could even speak clearly should he be offered the opportunity by King Artaxerxes.

As the door opened, Nehemiah squared his shoulders. *Stand tall,* he told himself. *If the Lord God so chooses, you will find favor at the right moment. And should that time come, you will be given the word to speak.* With this in mind, Nehemiah entered the presence of Artaxerxes, who in turn gave his cupbearer a quizzical look.

Nehemiah discerned King Artaxerxes' expression but pretended not to notice. Carefully, he placed the chalice of wine at the king's left, as he did each evening. Nehemiah then nodded with respect to Artaxerxes' queen, who quietly acknowledged the gesture.

As was his custom, Nehemiah then took one step backward, awaiting the king's response. Sometimes, Artaxerxes would simply send him on his way. At others however, the king might ask a question pertaining to a royal decision weighing on his mind, or engage his loyal subject in small talk to pass the time as he ate. Either way, Nehemiah knew not to speak without a directive from the King.

Nehemiah stood, trying to remain calm even as the tension inside him mounted. Artaxerxes' questioning countenance turned into a deep gaze as his eyes narrowed, boring into Nehemiah. Nehemiah held his breath for a moment, then, realizing he was giving off a sign of nervousness by doing so, tried to exhale slowly, as if this day was like any other. He tried to force a smile, with little success in his effort.

Artaxerxes took a sip of wine then placed the chalice back in its accustomed location. Reclining, the king folded his arms, never taking his eyes off of Nehemiah. After what seemed like an eternity, Artaxerxes spoke. "Why is your face sad though you are not sick? This is nothing but sadness of the heart."

Fear struck Nehemiah. The king *knew*. But how? Nehemiah struggled for a moment, trying to come up with the right words. As he struggled however, a thought struck him. *If the Lord has given the king my thoughts, can He not give me the words to say?*

After taking another deep breath, Nehemiah felt strength build inside him. He *knew* what he was going to say. He had been praying for this moment for months and the Lord would not let him down now.

With more power than he believed possible at a time like this, Nehemiah nodded once again to the queen, then turned back to Artaxerxes. "Let the king live forever," he said with a voice of calm. "Why should my face not be sad when the city, the place of my fathers' tombs, lies desolate and its gates have been consumed by fire?"

Nehemiah stiffened, awaiting a response. Would he be dismissed from the room? Banished to prison? Whatever his fate, Nehemiah knew one thing: The words he had spoken were from God. He could live with that. And he could die if necessary, knowing he had followed God's will.

Artaxerxes paused for a moment, thinking. He turned to his queen and gave her a hint of a smile before re-focusing his attention on Nehemiah. "What would you request?"

Nehemiah wondered about the meaning of the look from Artaxerxes to his queen. Was he walking into a trap? He didn't think so, but he had no way of knowing for sure. A king with confidence in his cupbearer one day could demand his execution the next.

For a moment, Nehemiah prayed quietly. *Lord God, this is the opportunity You have given. May my words be Yours. Now.*

Suddenly, confidence bubbled up in Nehemiah. The Lord, he knew, was on his side. A king was in front of him, certainly. But the One who could part seas and stop time, the One who ruled over all kings, was with him. Nehemiah's words were more direct now. "If it please the king, and if your servant has found favor before you, send me to Judah, to the city of my fathers' tombs, that I may rebuild it."

Nehemiah looked for a clue in the king's eyes. What was he thinking? He didn't have to wait long for an answer.

"How long will your journey be, and when will you return?" King Artaxerxes was leaning forward now, engaged.

The plan began to unfold in Nehemiah's mind, as if a blueprint for success had abruptly fallen from the heavens and into his arms. Without having to think, Nehemiah spoke. "If it please the king, let letters be given me for the governors of the provinces beyond the River; that they may allow me to pass through until I come to Judah."

Nehemiah wasn't finished. Without waiting for the king's reply, he pressed on. "And a letter to Asaph the keeper of the king's forest, that he may give me timber to make beams for the gates of the fortress which is by the temple, for the wall of the city and for the house to which I will go."

For a moment, Nehemiah was stunned. *Did I just say that? Did I just ask for a leave of absence, safe passage* **and** *timber from the king's forest?* Nehemiah looked down, suppressing a smile. The Lord's hand *was* on him, there was no question anymore.

Nehemiah's second key to the Wall of Hope: Dedication

Nehemiah was not a person to get excited about an idea one day and move on to something else the next. His four months of prayer and waiting on God showed powerful dedication to his calling. Because of his ability to hold on to his vision, when the timing was right he was more than prepared to speak directly to King Artaxerxes. Nehemiah didn't shrink when his moment arrived. With boldness he asked for the time and resources to rebuild the Wall of Jerusalem.

To succeed in our mission to turn our culture toward life, it is not necessary that we have the smartest, the wealthiest, or the most socially-connected. While God can use any of these attributes (for instance, Nehemiah had quite a connection with the king), what He needs most is our dedication.

God needs those who will stay the course even when times are challenging, even when the wisdom of this world tells us our culture is too far gone, that those who oppose us are too powerful and that we will never amass enough resources to complete our mission.

The dedicated don't have time for this kind of talk. Instead, they continue to pray. They get up every morning and keep trying. Instead of whimpering over the obstacles, they find solutions.

Nehemiah was dedicated. As a result, he saw that in spite of the challenges, the timing was right for him to lead the rebuilding effort.

I'm convinced that if we are dedicated, now is the right time for us to complete our Wall of Hope. Why? Because God has a tendency to do his greatest works when the odds are stacked against Him. One example of this of course, is Nehemiah. After 93 years without any true protection against their enemies, I doubt the Jewish people were thinking, "Hey let's rebuild that wall." Instead, they were likely terribly discouraged as they saw the rubble around them. In fact, as they went to bed each night they might have been wondering if they would wake up to a siege from a surrounding enemy.

After 40 years of Roe, we need Nehemiah's dedication, and we need it now because this is *just the right time* for God to work through His people in a miraculous way. Think about it: The current President of the United States is the first in history to keynote a gala for America's largest abortion provider, Planned Parenthood. Concluding his remarks, he told those gathered, "God bless Planned Parenthood."

Yes, this is a perfect time for God to show up and empower His people to do the impossible. But as we pointed out earlier, Nehemiah had to say, "Yes." We must do the same. For if we wait on others, we may find ourselves waiting a long time to change the world around us.

Dedication. A dedication that is unafraid of challenges. That's what we need, because now is the time to build our Wall of Hope.

And yet, along with Desire and Dedication, we need one more key.

Chapter 5
First Impressions, Facing the Challenges
(Nehemiah 2:11-15)

Darkness enshrouded Jerusalem as Nehemiah awoke early with eyes wide open, ready to get started. The sun would not show its presence for hours; there was plenty of time for his inspection of the wall.

Nehemiah stepped quietly outside his temporary home, looking for signs of life among the people. No one was stirring; which was perfect. He had told no one in Jerusalem of his plans, not yet. That would have to wait until he knew more, until the timing was right.

A nearby well offered water for his covert journey. Splashing the cool liquid on his face, Nehemiah prayed quietly. "No matter what I see, give me strength," he said to the Lord. "Your hand is upon me, let me never forget that."

Quietly mounting his mule, Nehemiah slipped out by the Valley Gate, in the direction of the Dragon's Well and toward the Refuse Gate. As he began his trek, discouragement crept in. Hoping that he would see some sign of rebuilding, any sign at all, Nehemiah's optimism was constantly dashed with stunning pictures of a stark reality.

Nothing. No signs of rebuilding. Anywhere.

Riding beside the wall, Nehemiah would nudge a brick here or there, sending it tumbling to the ground. At one point, while trying to push off of the wall with his foot, he almost lost his balance as timber and brick crumbled with even the slightest pressure.

In some areas, there was no wall at all. Nehemiah wondered how the people inside had survived this long. Over there, a semblance of what used to be a gate, now consumed by fire. And here, a breach so large an army could file through ten abreast.

Nehemiah passed on to the Fountain Gate, then to the King's Pool but could go no further due to rough terrain. Changing course, he rode up to the ravine where he stopped, folding his arms as he scanned the wall in front of him. The wall, everywhere, was in shambles. Anger burned inside of Nehemiah as, wherever he could see in the darkness, a ghastly picture of destruction overwhelmed him.

"Do they not care at all?" Nehemiah whispered to himself with quiet rage. "Generations since the return and not one effort to rebuild?" Nehemiah dismounted and shoved a brick lying on the ground, sending it tumbling down a small hill. He shook his head as he realized that portions of the brick remained between his toes, pieces of a crumbling remnant of what once stood tall.

As he considered this reality, Nehemiah began pacing beside the rubble that was once Jerusalem's fortress. At first, his gait was slow, deliberate. Looking down, Nehemiah spoke softly, reflectively. "This wall; it reflects a people who need rebuilding as well," he told himself. "This people must believe. Again."

Nehemiah harkened back to his encounter with Artaxerxes. If God could pierce the heart of a king with compassion for a people he did not know, what could God do for a people who once believed in Him? Was there a chance of reviving their faith?

Coming upon an old gate, Nehemiah stopped and stared. He could still see where flames once licked the timber. "Burned with fire," Nehemiah said in a whisper, echoing the words he heard months earlier when he first received the news. Hanani had been frighteningly accurate in his assessment.

Nehemiah thought of what that day must have been like, the day the flames tore through Jerusalem's wall. Did it burn for days? Did the last embers flicker for weeks?

And what of the faith of his people as they walked each day among these burned out walls, gates and towers? Had the fire of their faith finally been snuffed out? Or were there still flickering embers of a semblance of hope; looking for an opportunity to burn brightly once again?

As he turned back toward his mule, Nehemiah's mood turned toward determination. Now looking beyond the sad reality in front of him, Nehemiah shifted his focus toward the future. Again, he spoke quietly. But this time, there was certainty in his voice. "If we can just get started," Nehemiah thought aloud, "They will begin to believe. And if they believe, we can find a way."

Nehemiah stared down a hillside, zeroing in on another gaping breach. Taking a deep breath, Nehemiah pointed at the wall's open wound. "There," Nehemiah said with conviction. And though his only audience was his mule, he spoke with authority. "That is where we begin. This wall will stand tall once again. And as a people, we will stand as well."

As he stepped toward his mount, Nehemiah's stride was confident, purposeful. Hopping on his mule, he gave her an assuring pat. "Let's go," he told her. "We've got a job to do. Let's not waste any time."

Nehemiah's third key to our Wall of Hope: Determination

Nehemiah was a determined man, no question about it. He saw the challenges in front of him, certainly. But I think he had a vision for what needed to be done and something tells me that Nehemiah, in his mind's eye, actually *saw* the completed wall in all of its glory, even as the rubble of reality lay in front of him. More important, he could see a people turning back to the God they once knew; and he realized that the catalyst to this revival would be a wall, rising once again.

Nehemiah's vision led to a determination that would not be swayed by critics, setbacks or discouragement among the people. Ultimately, this determination was a key factor in his success.

Let's be honest and say that the vision we are talking about is monumental in scope. When we consider what it will take to literally shift our cultural landscape toward a society that values and protects the most innocent among us, we can count on critics. Setbacks, too. And yes, some among us will be discouraged and despairing at times. We're going to need determination and a lot of it.

Our mission is not for the faint of heart, nor for toy Christian soldiers. It is for those with Desire, Dedication and Determination. Nehemiah carried with him each of these attributes, yet we need to understand that *we are all capable of becoming a modern-day Nehemiah.*

Nehemiah saw a challenge and met that challenge. We can, too.

Nehemiah shook the world around him. We can, too.

Nehemiah gave a people hope. We can, too.

Nehemiah turned a people back to the God they once knew. We can, too.

And I believe that once we see our Wall of Hope, and what we can accomplish by completing this Wall, we will seize our moment, just like Nehemiah.

Let's take a journey to our Wall. I've seen it. I want you to see it, too . . .

Chapter 6
A Personal Journey to the Wall of Hope

All of us can make the choice to become a modern-day Nehemiah and take our place on the Wall of Hope across this country. Our first step is to clearly see our Wall, and find where it needs further strength. Then, we need to understand what its completion will mean, both for those who run inside and find safety, and for our country.

In order to see the Wall with clarity, we do not need a burning bush moment or a direct call from God. In Nehemiah's situation, God was only looking for the right heart. From there, God placed in Nehemiah the desire to rebuild and showed Nehemiah the pathway to success.

Nor do we need a spectacular story of conversion to the cause of life in order to take our place on the Wall. Those stories are often riveting, certainly. Honestly, I love to hear them. And in many cases, these stories stir others to action. But as you read, keep in mind that time and again, God uses ordinary people; people like Nehemiah, people like you, and people like me.

Walking through the Old Testament, we see that Abraham was too old. Moses had a stutter. David was the youngest son of Jesse, not the first-born. In the New Testament, Mary was too young, Peter too brash. Matthew was a tax-collector, Paul (once Saul) was too angry, and Mark deserted the ministry. But God found in their hearts all He needed to change the world.

If our hearts are focused on the love of God, our story,

whatever it is, is vital to building our Wall of Hope. We don't have to be famous. We don't have to be outgoing or persuasive or clever. We simply need to be willing.

This is precisely why I share my story. Mine is a story of fears, flaws and failures. But this is also a story of what God can do with those of us who, even with our struggles, care enough to try and make a difference.

Stirrings

In the fall of 1980 I was a new Christian and a college freshman at Auburn University in Alabama. There, I got to know two pastors who stood strong on their belief in the sanctity of human life. These pastors were of different denominations, yet they shared a Biblical world view and were close friends as well.

I'd love to relate a watershed moment here, a particular circumstance or life experience that forever placed me in the pro-life camp, but there is none. All I can relate here is this: the influence of those two pastors was so great that over several months during that freshman year in the fall of 1980, I became convinced that part of my mission in life was to play a role in creating a culture of life in this country.

My prayer was basic: I asked God to place me on the front line in defending life.

Finding the front line

Initially, I believed my future in pro-life work would revolve around public policy and politics. Because 1980 was an election year, this seemed to make perfect sense. Though at the time I wasn't considering Nehemiah and his wall as a model, I would have seen my political efforts as the most effective way to build a Wall of Hope. I got involved in every campaign I could find, believing we were just one election away from ending abortion.

You and I both know it didn't happen that way. Some pro-life candidates won, some lost. The Supreme Court shifted slightly, but Roe remained the law of the land.

A first view of the Wall of Hope

Ten years later, in 1991 I was a husband and father of one, engaging myself in political endeavors at night while working in sales during the day. One evening however, I got an interesting phone call from a close friend, who served as executive director of our local pregnancy help center. These ministries go by many names today, but back in 1991 they were termed "crisis pregnancy centers;" and were mostly small, mom and pop-sized organizations trying to make a difference in the lives of those facing unplanned pregnancies.

The moment I heard the voice on the other end, I recall sensing that my life was about to change. I knew he was leaving our local center to take a similar position in a larger, metropolitan area. Days earlier, when I heard he was going to make the move, I remember saying, "I would hate to be the person who has to try and fill his shoes." In my mind, he was a legend (and still is). Replacing him would be next to impossible, and I didn't think about it further.

Yet as soon as I heard his voice, I knew why he was calling and I dreaded it. He was asking a few friends to consider applying for his soon-to-be vacant position. Years earlier I had asked him for advice on how to get more involved in the pro-life movement and he gave me good counsel, so his call was not a surprise.

Still, I could not see why anyone would think I was a fit for the job. The center was pro-life, of course. But it was also evangelistic, and I had no real ministry background. At this point in my life, my Biblical teaching experience was limited to teaching a Sunday school class for two-year-olds. While I was adept at fetching juice and crackers or telling the story of Zaccheus (and a wee little man was he), I wasn't sure how this would translate to a pregnancy help center.

In addition, I was quite young for such a role. As a brand new father, I was hardly equipped to impart wisdom to parents of children facing unplanned pregnancies.

If this weren't enough to disqualify me, I had little knowledge of how the center actually operated. When I thought about it, I could not remember ever walking in the door.

And there was another reason for my reticence: my prayer ten years earlier was to be placed on the *front* line, not in what I considered to be a fledgling organization with minimum impact on the big picture. I wanted to be in Washington, D.C. or in a major public policy institute. But a crisis pregnancy center? I had not even considered the idea.

Still, I agreed to apply. I didn't see where there was anything to lose. When asked to a first interview, I went with few expectations.

Yet somewhere during that first interview with the board, I became intrigued with the idea of serving with this bunch. While a pregnancy help center wasn't necessarily the place where I saw myself long-term, something told me that here, in this 1200-square foot space, God was doing something.

Was this the front line for which I had prayed? At that moment, I didn't think so. But I could not deny the fact that my heart was growing toward this center and its people. For reasons I could not understand or properly explain, in that one interview my line of thinking shifted from a cavalier attitude to a desperate desire to join this center be a part of what it was accomplishing.

Still, in my mind I was totally inadequate for the task. And during the third and final interview I was at least transparent enough to say so. When asked by the board if I had a particular weakness, I offered not one but two.

"I'm not good at fundraising," I told them frankly. "Asking people for funds just isn't comfortable for me." Second, I had a fear. "I also know that speaking in public; at churches and at our events, is something I would have to do," I said. "I'm not good at it. Just the thought of speaking in front of people is petrifying."

They hired me anyway. And on my first day on the job, an incredible journey began. I didn't know it at the time, but inside the doors of that center was the front line I was looking for. In addition, I would begin to see the Wall of Hope under construction.

At that time most pregnancy help centers had little more than a few dollars and a lot of heart. Our budget, with two full-time and one part-time staff member, was less than $70,000. Thankfully, we had several dozen outstanding volunteers who were the heartbeat of our center. We offered free pregnancy testing, a listening ear, mentoring for moms and dads, and attempted to meet as many material needs as possible. In addition, we had volunteer physicians, nurses and lab technicians, allowing us to offer free prenatal care up to 20 weeks of pregnancy.

We had plenty of joyful moments at our center during my time there. One of the greatest was seeing those who chose life bring smiling babies in our door; babies who might never have drawn a first breath without the work and help of so many who were involved with the center.

We had sorrows, too. I'll never forget the parents who told me that if their daughter, a college student, chose to carry her child to term, they would pull every dime of support for her education. They won the battle and a child lost his, or her, life.

Still, the victories far outnumbered the tragedies. There was the young lady who battled emotional struggles throughout her pregnancy far beyond what I could imagine; yet during this time made a faith decision to follow Jesus Christ. Later, she chose adoption for her child and went on to volunteer with a Christian adoption agency.

And there is the memory of the girl who told me point-blank, "I'm going to have an abortion. Tomorrow."

My response was simple: "I don't think you will, but no matter what your decision is, we will be here if you need us." Four months later she returned, asking for maternity clothes. She chose life.

And these stories, of which there are literally hundreds, are only a few snapshots from a gallery of lives changed and lives saved. With a dedicated group committed to each other and to those who came in our door, we watched the center expand in ways we could not have dreamed. We were a team, and surprisingly to me, a powerful one.

I'd love to tell you here that my leadership fueled our success, but the truth is I had many flaws. I wasn't a great manager of people or office systems; often grappling endlessly with even the simplest of decisions. But the people I had the joy of working with were incredibly loving and so engaged in reaching out to those who came in our door that we grew in spite of my inexperience and struggles.

Honestly, the more I think of those years the more I think of my shortcomings. There is a reason however, why I share these weaknesses: All of us have imperfections; reasons why we can say, "Not me. I'm not capable of taking part in all of this."

Right here I could pen a volume on why I was unequipped, too weak or simply not good enough to be a part of that center, much less to be seen as its *leader*. We have a choice to either look at our flaws and say, "no," or to follow our hearts and serve in whatever capacity God asks of us. The one thing I know I did *right* was to step forward and try. Any of us can do that much.

As a center, we began to grow—quickly. Our number of new clients grew to more than 100 each month, our budget expanded to more than $100,000 and then beyond $200,000. And in 1996 our center joined a few other PHCs in adding a new initiative: Ultrasound. With this tool, women unsure about carrying their babies to term could actually *see* their children before making a final decision.

As a result, our center grew even more. The prayer I had voiced years earlier was coming to fruition. Finally, I was on the front line in protecting life.

A different road

Yet in 1997, just as our center seemed headed to new heights, everything changed in my personal life. My wife suddenly abandoned our family, leaving me emotionally wrecked. I was left to raise three children, ages 7, 5 and 3; on my own. While I sought every avenue available to save our marriage, nothing worked.

Honesty compels me to admit I was broken on every front imaginable. I saw myself as a failure as a husband and as a father. Not only that, I believed that I was no longer qualified to work with Christian organizations.

I was prepared to resign from the center more than once but our board of directors insisted I stay. In 1999 however, I knew my children needed me at home. I stepped down, wondering if I would ever be involved in PHC work again. My dream to be on the front line of protecting life was, in my mind, virtually over.

What about you? Is there some reason why you might believe God can no longer use you? Is there a past decision or situation that makes you wonder whether you can make a difference? This is exactly what I thought. But even as God saw the crumbled road of my life, He began to forge a new path for me. My pastor has said many times, "The plan of God can sometimes be thwarted, but no one can stop God's planning ability." My life is a case in point. Yours might be an example as well.

To try and stay connected to the pregnancy help center movement and stay close to my children, I launched a home-based company I called LifeTrends. Using my journalism background I created a publication for pregnancy help centers offering ideas and articles for their center newsletters, called *LifeTrends Monthly*. A couple of hundred centers signed up, giving me an opportunity to stay in touch with these organizations.

With three children and with LifeTrends only providing a part-time income however, money was an issue. And yet it seemed God opened another door at just the right time. When I called the headmaster of my children's Christian school to inform him that I could no longer afford tuition, he stopped me. "Bring them anyway, Kirk. We'll work something out."

On the first day of school, the headmaster called. "Our receptionist is under the weather. Can you fill in?" I most certainly could.

A few days later he called again. "Would you be interested in our public relations position? I can offer you a first-year teacher's salary and lower your children's tuition by half." I accepted without reservation. Within a few weeks my role expanded to Director of Development and within a month, I was serving as coordinator for the school's new million-dollar capital campaign.

Other doors opened as well. I got a call from a national organization specializing in training pregnancy help centers on how to implement effective fundraising events. They asked me to join their team of national consultants, and in addition, enlisted me to re-write several training manuals for them. A new road was unfolding.

This opportunity was a gift from God in many ways. Our school's headmaster was beyond exceptional; as an educator, an executive and as a friend. With my office just a few feet away from his door, I learned something each day about leadership and in particular, servant leadership. This position also afforded me something I never dreamed of: The chance to be near my children during a difficult time in their lives. During the day I was within a few steps of my children and at night we were all home together as I began building relationships with PHCs around the country through LifeTrends.

So just nine months after leaving my position as executive director of a pregnancy help center, I now had three jobs which, in the aggregate, took care of our financial needs. And though the schedule was hectic at times, I could still be a dad.

In addition, these three opportunities created a path that ultimately led to this book.

First, by working on the school's million-dollar capital campaign I was learning principles on how to connect with those people with a heart to give. Back then, I had no idea that today God would be using those skills to help me design capital campaigns for PHCs all over the country, including one center's $7 million vision for the future.

Second, through my work with the national consulting group I was seeing the inside of PHCs all over America. From California to Florida, Massachusetts to Texas and anywhere in between, I got to view the strengths and challenges of these centers.

Third, LifeTrends, my company, gave me insight into the needs of PHCs. Because I was emailing and talking to directors, staff and board members of PHCs of all shapes and sizes, my eyes were opened to the possibilities in front of these organizations.

And yet, there was more to come. Within another year or so I was asked to serve as the keynote speaker at a fundraising dinner for a PHC in Wyoming. Though I still feared public speaking, my nine years as an executive director gave me so many opportunities to stand in front of people that the nerves began to calm (well, a little). It was time to share my passion for these centers in a larger setting.

The Wyoming event went better than expected and the next thing I knew I was taking on engagements all over, to the point where I eventually asked the school to alter my contract so I could speak at more events. My headmaster graciously agreed.

To make things work I was often on a tight schedule. I recall dropping my children at school one Thursday morning and heading straight to the Atlanta airport for an event in Pittsburgh. My mother picked up the three kids for a Thursday night stay over at her house while I spoke that evening. On Friday I took the first flight out of Pittsburgh to Atlanta and drove back to the school. By 9:45 in the morning I was at my desk. My Friday wrapped up with a high school football game, twelve hours later.

Speaking engagements offered me a fourth view of the Wall of Hope. In preparation for these events I would spend time with the executive director, staff and board; asking about the PHC's challenges and its vision for the future. In addition I almost always got the chance to visit the center on the day of the event, walking through every room and hearing the stories of what was going on inside the walls of the center. This gave me a unique, insider's perspective on PHCs and the Wall they are building.

I could not have asked for a better situation.

I need to pause here. As you are reading, you are seeing how pieces fell into place for me and my children to not only survive, but to thrive. And you can also see where God took my desire to remain involved in PHC work and through opportunities I could have never created on my own, made it happen. Though I was no longer on the front line, I was now supplying support, encouragement, and the critical tools needed to assist those on the front line.

In the end, God took my experiences and allowed me to accomplish more than I could have ever dreamed.

And as if all of those blessings weren't enough, in 2005 I met Jennifer. In the years since my marriage ended I had dated, but was beginning to believe I would not be married again. In fact, one of my daughters, then 13-years-old, told me not to worry about bringing a mother figure into her life. "Daddy," she told me, "the four of us are just fine. I don't think we need anyone else." We had made it on our own for more than nine years and perhaps I needed to forget about adding someone to their lives, or mine.

Yet through a series of events I can only explain as God-inspired, Jennifer and I connected. The moment I first saw her smile, I was hooked. Though she lived more than five hours away in Nashville, TN, the distance didn't seem to matter to either of us.

It was as if God saw not only Jennifer and me, but my three children as well, and knew we needed to be a family. Jennifer had a heart to not only be my mate, but also to pour into the kids those things they lost over the years.

Though we had originally planned to live in Alabama, the children wanted a fresh start and we moved to the Nashville area, where we live today. The move allowed me to make LifeTrends a full-time endeavor, and opened doors to expand my speaking schedule. Our story however, doesn't end there. Since our marriage, Jennifer and I have added two more Waldens to the bunch, bringing our quiver to five.

Devoting all of my time to LifeTrends made a huge difference. PHCs began calling, asking for consulting on visionary planning. Statewide PHC networks and national affiliate organizations allowed me to lead conferences and provide workshops on a myriad of PHC -related issues.

The growth did not end there. In 2009, Heartbeat International, the world's largest PHC affiliate network, asked if I would consider a partnership. Through this relationship with Heartbeat, LifeTrends' flagship publication, *The LifeTrends Connection,* now reaches more than 1,500 pregnancy help centers each month.

Looking back over these past thirteen years since launching LifeTrends, I can say that while I haven't viewed the inside of *every* PHC, I've seen more than a representative sample from all areas of the country. LifeTrends and my speaking opportunities have taken me through more than 85 airports and into virtually every state in the Union. In a nine-week period one fall, I traveled more than 33,000 miles.

Ordinary people with an extraordinary God

There is another take away from my story. All of this began with a simple prayer from a college freshman in 1980: "Lord, put me on the front line in protecting life."

It is a prayer answered, beyond what I could have imagined as I began my first days of college. Like all of our journeys, mine has its twists and turns, yet God found a way to take an ordinary person and help him see an extraordinary Wall of Hope that has the capacity to literally transform our culture.

To me, what is most interesting about this story is that in spite of our own weaknesses and struggles, God can make a way to accomplish His plan.

Today I look back and see that God took a young man who said he could not speak in public, and has now placed him in front of literally tens of thousands of people at hundreds of events to . . . speak in public.

And God looked at a guy who said he was nervous about trying to raise funds, and has allowed him to be a part of raising more than $25 million for PHCs across the country over the last decade.

It is a reminder that where we are weak, God is stronger than we can imagine.

On top of that, God looked at a broken man; a man who believed he was washed out of Christian work, and rebuilt him into someone who now enjoys the incredible blessing of partnering with hundreds and hundreds of such Christ-centered organizations and ministries.

We are all ordinary people. We have our flaws, our weaknesses, our fears . . . and yet we also have our hopes and our dreams. Our God knows them all.

God uses ordinary people. I'm certainly proof of that.

And I am convinced that God continues to use ordinary people to accomplish the extraordinary mission of saving the lives of His littlest ones. And I believe God's greatest work in this area is about to take place.

In fact, I believe our Wall of Hope is halfway to completion. Looking back at our friend Nehemiah, he had a moment where he came to the same conclusion.

Chapter 7
Nehemiah's Wall and Ours:
"Half its Height"

Nehemiah finished his daily inspection of the wall and looked for a place of solitude. Spotting a hillside with a shady fig tree, he trudged over and settled underneath, nearly exhausted.

"Sanballat. He is constantly mocking us," Nehemiah told the Lord. "And if I'm not hearing his drivel, Tobiah steps up with even worse on his tongue."

Nehemiah silently recalled Tobiah's latest proclamation: "Even what they are building—if a fox should jump on it, he would break their stone wall down!" Nehemiah shook his head in disgust, asking the Lord to remember the deeds of those like Sanballat and Tobiah who sought to disrupt the work.

Looking back at the wall, Nehemiah rubbed his tired eyes and surveyed. Something was . . . different. He glanced around, trying to figure out what he was missing. Was there a breach? Was someone not in place? Was a family missing?

Nehemiah closed his dark brown eyes, clasping his head with his hands, trying to think. "What is it?" he whispered to himself. He went through his mental checklist of tasks, duties and of the progress made to this point. Nothing came to mind.

Opening his eyes and gazing up and down what he could see of the structure in front of him, Nehemiah rested his chin on his fists and tried to concentrate. He focused on the wall a second time, then a third. Finally, it hit him. Something *was* different.

Nodding his head, Nehemiah's countenance took on a look of

satisfaction. For the first time, he could see *no* breaches at all. Not one. Everything—all of the mortar and the brick—was joined together. No, the wall wasn't finished. But even through the mocking, the fears and the threats; this people had pushed on and now, the foundation was clearly in place.

"Halfway," Nehemiah told himself. He stood, placing his hands on his hips. A sense of triumph enveloped him and a joy spread across his face. "Let Tobiah continue to taunt us," Nehemiah told himself. "But when this wall is completed, his mocking will turn to respect, for this people and for this wall. And that day is coming soon. Very soon."

> *So we built the wall and the whole wall was joined together to half its height, for the people had a mind to work.*
> *— Nehemiah 4:6*

When I first started working in a PHC ministry in 1991, I had no idea of the foundation being built not only in our center, but in hundreds of similar centers throughout the country. Now there are more than 2500 of these centers, going by many names:

> Pregnancy Help Center
> Pregnancy Care Center
> Pregnancy Resource Center
> Pregnancy Help Medical Clinic
> Pregnancy Care Clinic
> Pregnancy Assistance Center
> Crisis Pregnancy Center

A PHC might also carry the name of one of two national affiliate networks; either Heartbeat International or CareNet.

These centers are solidly joined together in mission and purpose. And the Wall, in its foundational stages back in the early 90s, is now built to half its height. Twenty years ago, funding wasn't available to provide much more than a few offerings and programs. But today? The pregnancy help center that could offer only free pregnancy tests years ago might now provide:

- Ultrasound, with experienced medical personnel

- Fatherhood initiatives to mentor new dads

- Couples counseling, mentoring and support

- Relationship and abstinence education initiatives for public and private schools, church youth groups and college students

- Testing for Sexually Transmitted Infections and Diseases (STIs and STDs) along with expert counsel on the benefits of waiting until marriage before entering a physical relationship

- Parenting education

- Adoption information and referral

- Job skills training

- Post-Abortion Recovery initiatives focusing on the power of God's forgiveness for past decisions

- Continuing education

- Professional counseling for various needs ranging from marriage issues to sexual abuse

Of the hundreds of centers I've had an opportunity to see, the overwhelming majority are hardly mom and pop operations. These are first-class, professional organizations always looking to the cutting edge.

For instance, in the Midwest I visited a center where they not only provide prenatal care, but well-baby care up to a year, at no charge to clients.

A center in the Southwest has a high school for new moms and dads. The year I visited they graduated twelve students and *all* went on to college. More examples?

How about the center on the East Coast that created an abstinence-based education initiative for schools that was so effective, the teen pregnancy rate in its county dropped more than 40% in two years?

We might also look at a center in the West that opened a medical clinic with ultrasound and within a year, the abortion rate in its county dropped by 43%.

Or the center where one room resembled a New York City boutique, full of executive clothing for women. Why? Because the center offers classes on job seeking and makes certain that each graduate is dressed for success when meeting with a prospective employer.

We're told that a first impression is important and I'm finding PHCs where even the most discerning design critic could walk into the lobby and say, "Now, *this* is nice!" These facilities are not opulent, but because every dollar is used effectively, many PHCs present themselves to clients with incredible distinction.

Look in the ultrasound room at many of these centers and you'll find a flat-screen, high-definition television, offering clients a detailed and awe-inspiring view of their babies. Talk to the nurses and you'll find professionals who know their craft and perform their callings with excellence.

Twenty years ago almost all of this would have been unheard of. Hiring nurses? Purchasing $40,000 ultrasound machines? Medical services? Far-off dreams of years ago are now reality.

And these centers are reaching more people than ever, including dads. In one Midwestern state I talked with the founder of a fatherhood initiative who told me his PHC had more than 25 dads whom he and others were mentoring. In his community, marriage is a nearly forgotten word. And yet, this man is changing the culture and building marriage once again. Four of these fathers were getting married in the coming months.

Married dads are better dads. They are closer to their children and their children are more likely to escape poverty, legal troubles and future unplanned pregnancies.

This is happening all over America at pregnancy help centers. The foundation is in place. The wall is at half its height. All we need to do is keep building.

Let's say it again: Ours is a Wall of protection not only for children, but for mothers and fathers as well. Inside this Wall, young men and women are finding hope, and also discovering practical ways to meet the challenges they face.

As a result, lives are being saved. And, many who come in the doors of PHCs across the country are making faith decisions to follow Jesus Christ. These decisions not only build better families today; they also build legacies of strong families for generations to come.

This Wall of Hope PHCs are creating is vital because we

understand that moms and dads don't go to abortion centers because they see it as a good choice. In fact, most realize going into the abortion clinic that they will regret their decision. But they go because they see no other option.

Pregnancy help centers *are* that option. And as these centers become the first choice for more and more, the attractiveness of the second choice—abortion—diminishes. And we know that every time parents choose life, an abortion center somewhere loses income. When enough of that income disappears . . . the abortion center closes its doors.

Take the following piece of information from someone who has seen the inside of hundreds and hundreds of PHCs:

Pregnancy help centers are quietly and consistently building the Wall of Hope. The foundation is now in place for exponential growth. Today this foundation is halfway home to becoming a completed Wall. There is more to be done, but not as much as we might think.

Chapter 8
From Foundation to Completion

"Sir, a message," said the boy, nearly breathless, as he ran to the base of the wall and looked up to Nehemiah. Nehemiah turned to the boy slowly, knowing that Sanballat and Tobiah, enemies of the wall, sent the young messenger and were somewhere out there, watching for his reaction. He would give them no satisfaction. Nehemiah eased the cumbersome brick off of his shoulder and began settling it into place, taking his time.

With his massive arms glistening from perspiration in the morning sunlight, Nehemiah eyed his visitor. He guessed the youngster to be about fourteen or fifteen, and he sensed the boy's fear. The messenger was likely wondering whether Nehemiah might use this as an opportunity to retaliate.

Nehemiah chuckled quietly to himself, shaking his head. The boy was safe; but the lad was likely too young to realize it. Nehemiah slowly finished tucking the brick into position as he prepared to reset one of the city's gates. *What does Sanballat have for me today?* He wondered.

Nehemiah was hardly worried. The verbal attacks from his foes came almost daily, but since the moment he realized the wall was half its height, Nehemiah no longer concerned himself over whether the job would be completed. Now, it was just a matter of time. Nehemiah's confidence was brimming now. And more important, the confidence of his people was returning too.

Nehemiah, arms crossed and standing on the top of the wall,

smiled at the young messenger looking up to him. "What is your word from Sanballat, young man?" Nehemiah asked.

The boy's voice wavered. "From, uh, Geshem also, sir," the lad said, trying to compose himself. "Both Sanballat and Geshem. They have a . . . a . . . a message for you." The boy was fumbling, trying to find his voice.

Nehemiah nodded. "So the two of them have bravely sent you, have they?"

The boy's eyes were wide with awe. After a long silence, he found the strength to speak again: "They say to you, 'Come; let us meet together at Chephirim in the plain of Ono.'"

Nehemiah slowly stood, taking in the message with an eye to the horizon. Nehemiah figured they were to the West, hiding out of view behind one of the many boulders dotting the landscape.

Nehemiah noted the irony of the moment. Only days earlier these same men were openly mocking the work; today they were hiding. Could they see him? Nehemiah didn't care.

Nehemiah knew the proposed meeting was a trap. Did those two think he was so naïve? To Nehemiah, the only question was whether they wanted to capture him or kill him. They would do neither; Nehemiah knew that much.

Nehemiah gazed across the top of the wall, considering his reply. *So they are worried now, are they?*

Nehemiah answered the boy calmly, yet firmly. "Tell sirs Sanballat and Geshem that in due time I will send my messengers with my reply." The lad dashed away quickly while Nehemiah turned back to the project in front of him, carefully inspecting his work. He was in no rush to answer anyone, much less those two.

So I sent messengers to them, saying "I am doing a great work, and I cannot come down. Why should the work stop while I leave it and come down to you?"
—Nehemiah 6:3

Nehemiah's tormenters—Sanballat and Geshem—sought to pull him off of the wall (Neh. 6:1-2). But Nehemiah would have none of it. Interestingly, Nehemiah 6:4 notes that these enemies sent messages to Nehemiah four times, and each time, Nehemiah answered them "in the same way": he was not leaving his mission until it was finished.

He didn't have time to get into arguments and fruitless discussions over why he was staying on the wall. He had a job to do and nothing was going to come between Nehemiah and the completion of his God-given task.

It's the same situation for the many of us who believe in the sanctity of life. We understand there are those who seek to distract us. We need look no further than groups like the abortion goliath, Planned Parenthood. They, The National Abortion and Reproductive Rights Action League (NARAL), The National Organization for Women (NOW) and others seek to pull us off of our Wall with media campaigns, public relations blitzes, lawsuits and more.

They want to discourage us. They want to slow us down. Most of all, they want us to come down from our Wall and ultimately, they want us to give up on our mission.

Our plan should be just like Nehemiah's. First, we will trust God and in His provision for us.

Second, we will go to work and build our Wall. Let our enemies have at it. We are not going to whimper or whine; we are not going to cower in fear. We are going to build.

Our Wall is going to be strong, and we will stand on that Wall. And we will invite inside our Wall the hurting, the fearful, the desperate and the destitute. We are not going to back down. And we are not going to back up or let up.

They will mock us. And we will build the Wall.

They will attack us. And we will build the Wall.

Like Nehemiah, we have no time to come down from our Wall and chat. We are close to completion. Here is just how close:

Thirty years ago, we would have likely found only a few hundred PHCs. Yet the number of abortion centers at that time was as many as 2,000 or more.

But things have changed. As we mentioned earlier, there are now some 2500 PHCs throughout the United States. The number of abortion centers? The number is dropping, now less than 700 at this writing.

And just twenty years ago, few if any pregnancy help centers offered ultrasound services. Today an educated guess is that more than 1,000 PHCs offer ultrasound. And more add this service each month. PHC statistics indicate that of those women who see their children on an ultrasound screen, more than 90% choose *life*.

Not only that, more and more PHCs are incorporating mobile ultrasound. With RVs fully equipped with medical technology, these centers are taking ultrasound directly to areas close to abortion centers. Today it's not surprising to see an RV from a local PHC parked just steps away from an abortion facility, ready to reach out to those still considering their options.

And every month or so I hear another story of a pregnancy help center re-locating to the same street, the same block or even next door to an abortion center. These centers are beginning to level the playing field with the abortion industry by providing better facilities, brighter atmospheres and hope; creating a powerful contrast to those wanting, through abortion, to profit off of those facing a challenging pregnancy.

Not every pregnancy help center can offer medical services at this point, but this isn't slowing down the building of the Wall. Many PHCs are entering into strong partnerships with each other, connecting clients with ultrasound through a quick phone call. In addition, we're seeing pro-life physicians step into the picture, offering free ultrasounds to clients referred by their local PHCs.

Fatherhood initiatives are also building this Wall to new heights. In the Midwest a college football assistant coach works more than 20 hours each week with his local PHC, reaching out to young men through schools, events and more. A young man entering this center can walk into its lobby and within minutes, be talking with a man's man about the challenges he faces.

These initiatives for new dads are vital, because most women who choose abortion later say that if the child's father had been supportive of the pregnancy, they would have likely chosen life for their babies. In short, the fatherhood initiatives popping up in PHCs all over the United States may save thousands of lives.

We could extend this chapter dozens of pages if we began walking through example after example of a growing, strengthening Wall of Hope, built by PHCs. This Wall of Hope is creating story after story of changed lives . . .

Like the college football player, looking to be tested for a sexually transmitted disease, who found a PHC in the South. During his appointment he chose to end his road of promiscuity and took another step as well: He chose a relationship with Jesus Christ. He is now happily married and working with a national Christian ministry.

Or the young lady at a Big10 university who found herself pregnant through a sexual assault, yet still chose life for her child. She told an audience of several hundred how a PHC reached out to her, supported her and in the end, changed her life and brought her new hope.

And the young man who told a banquet audience that when his girlfriend was pregnant, the PHC stood beside him "And told me I was man enough to be a father. I'm going to be that man for my daughter, because they taught me how."

Friends, we may not realize it yet but we are starting to win. Victories are piling up. We are building this Wall of Hope. Completion is not somewhere out on the horizon; it is right in front of us.

When we complete our Wall of Hope, abortion in this country will decrease—rapidly. Will this tragedy be eliminated altogether? While it is nearly impossible to imagine, who knows what God might do with a people who are willing to build?

Chapter 9
Raising the Wall of Hope to Full Height

As the air of early evening cooled the dozen or so men walking inside of the wall of Jerusalem, Nehemiah stopped every few minutes to check portions of the work, asking questions as part of his daily inspection.

"This gate," he said to the tallest of those with him. "Secure?"

"Yes, sir. Try it."

Nehemiah made an attempt to pry the gate open. Then another. After a third attempt, he gave up with satisfaction. "Absolutely," he said.

He wasn't finished. Nehemiah pointed across a courtyard. "Over there. Are we at full height?"

From the back of the group came the reply: "Not only full height; we added several cubits there as well."

Nehemiah nodded. Despite the descending darkness, the warmth of hope built as he scrolled through his mental list from the day before. "What am I missing?" Nehemiah asked the group.

No one said a word.

Nehemiah scanned his memory for reminders of any gates, towers or other portions of the wall that were one day ago incomplete. Another question formed. "Are there any other areas where we are vulnerable?"

Again, none of the men responded. Several however, began looking at each other with knowing glances, then back to Nehemiah. He was their leader and they wanted to know if what they were beginning to realize was actually true.

Nehemiah wasn't finished. "We've reinforced the eastern portion, have we not?"

"We've doubled its thickness," said the young man next to Nehemiah. "I would stand on the wall and face any army." His voice was confident, assured.

"And the towers to the southwest. Are they ready?"

"King David himself would be proud of those towers, sir," an older gentleman said. "Laid many of the bricks and timber myself, along with my sons. They will stand tall. You have my word."

"I do not doubt it," Nehemiah responded with a nod of assurance.

Nehemiah stopped walking. Those with him halted as well. Nehemiah turned, facing the men. Their eyes locked on his.

"Men, our work here is . . ." Nehemiah paused for a moment as his voice started to crack. Even in the faint light, the men could see his eyes welling with tears. "This wall is finished." Nehemiah took a deep breath. "Completed."

Nehemiah continued. "There will be more to do, I assure you," he said. "But tonight, return to your families and share the news among all of Jerusalem. And let us celebrate among the people. The Wall is rebuilt and tonight, our Jerusalem . . . she is safe."

So the wall was completed on the twenty-fifth of the month Elul, in fifty-two days.

And it came about when all our enemies heard of it, and all the nations surrounding us saw it, they lost their confidence; for they recognized that this work had been accomplished with the help of our God.
—Nehemiah 6:15-16

In recent years I've begun to recognize the Wall of Hope; and now I see what its completion means.

Let me ask a question. What if you woke up one morning and heard the following on a cable TV news network?:

"The abortion center's closing is another in a long line of abortion providers leaving the industry, a trend that has grown in the last several years. The director here echoes the refrain we are hearing across the country: 'There were simply too few clients to keep the doors open.'"

That's exactly what will happen when we complete this Wall.

Consider that abortion centers, even the so-called "non-profit" entities like Planned Parenthood, need money to stay open. They must keep the funds rolling in and abortion is the cash cow of these operations. Without abortion, people don't get paid and sooner or later, the center must close its doors.

Let's look more closely at abortion's giant, Planned Parenthood. Yes, they receive our tax dollars. In 2011, Planned Parenthood's take of the federal pie was a whopping $542 million and under the current administration that amount will only rise.

But, Planned Parenthood's private donations were only $307.5 million in 2011-12, a slight drop in the last two years from $308.2 million in 2009-2010. When private donations fail to increase and the rest of Planned Parenthood's abortion income drops, the abortion-behemoth will be in big, big trouble because tax dollars won't be able to make up the shortfall.

The secret truth then, is that Planned Parenthood and other abortion-industry "Giants" are not giants at all. We view them as Goliaths because they appear to have all of the funding and power, giving a false perception of indestructibility.

In reality however, these organizations are only modern-day Sanballats, Tobiahs and Geshems, just as in Nehemiah's narrative. They've been given *some* power by others, but they can't control us. Though they will certainly try, they can't stop us from building our Wall of Hope.

The abortion industry has and will continue to attempt to use state legislatures to shut down the work of PHCs. They've made attempts in New York, California, Maryland, Oregon, Washington and in many other states. But guess what? PHCs are still on the Wall. And these centers are still building.

Nehemiah finished his wall in 52 days, a wall that protected about 50,000 people. The PHC Wall of Hope is designed to protect the approximately 1.2 million children lost to abortion each year, and their 2.4 million moms and dads. That's about 75 times the number of people protected by the Wall of Jerusalem, but there is every reason to believe that if we join forces with these centers, we can finish our mission, too.

For comparison's sake, if we take 52 days and multiply it by 75, completing our Wall of Hope would take 3,900 days or a little more than 10 years.

The foundation is in place. The Wall of Hope is rising. In just over 10 years, there is every reason why we can build this Wall to full height.

It's almost finished, and here is how we are going to complete our mission . . .

After more than 30 years of participation, observation and dedication to life-affirming principles, I may not have all of the answers but I've found a couple of more truths.

The first truth is this:

The best location for our Wall of Hope is pregnancy help centers standing side-by-side across the United States. Through these organizations and ministries, we can work toward dropping the U.S. abortion rate by 75% or more. Regardless of where we place ourselves in the spiritual battle for life; whether on the political front, the social action arena or elsewhere, we all have a stake in this Wall we can build through our PHCs.

The second:

After listening to, corresponding with, training, encouraging and supporting thousands of laborers in PHCs across America, I know that if we create a level playing field with those organizations aligned against life, we will see life win out much more often than we can imagine.

We will win because those facing unplanned pregnancies and those wanting answers on how to build healthy relationships are desperate for the solutions we offer. They need a place where they can find safety. That's what we are doing; we're almost there.

So how do we complete our Wall? When reading through Nehemiah's narrative we find that his endeavor involved not only a brick and mortar wall, but also the repairing of the wall's gates and towers. The gates provided an entrance and protection; the towers provided an observation point and sent a powerful message of strength. When we consider that every Wall of Hope needs not only the brick and mortar, but gates and towers as well, we see what we need to complete our mission:

We will create **Gates of Excellence** to provide a tremendous first-impression.

We will build the **Wall** to full height with strengthened staffing and services.

We will construct tall **Towers** to call everyone in need to the Wall of Hope.

Let's look at each of the three . . .

Chapter 10
The Best Facilities for Pregnancy Help Centers:
The Gates of Excellence of our Wall of Hope

Then Eliashib the high priest arose with his brothers the priests and built the
Sheep Gate; they consecrated it and hung its doors . . .
—Nehemiah 3:1A

Nehemiah understood how important gates can be; his narrative carefully describes the role of the priests in consecrating the Sheep Gate where the sacrifices would be brought in, and in other places we see certain gates bolted and locked for safety. For pregnancy help centers, gates are the entrance point, the first opportunity to tell those who enter; *your place of rest and refuge is inside.*

When the gates of a PHC are solid and strong, the first impression created is one of hope and comfort. For pregnancy help centers, their gates are defined by the various buildings, office complexes and homes where they serve their clients.

Many PHCs have facilities that are second to none. These gates create a perfect entrance point, sending a powerful message of distinction. When a client comes in and sees waiting areas and rooms that are bright, well-decorated and professional, she is much more likely to place her confidence in the pregnancy help center, and in those who serve her there.

This is exactly what we need for our gates. For a client who is scared and unsure, a positive first impression is one of the most effective avenues for reaching her heart. When I see a waiting room that is inviting and warm, I see opportunities for success in sharing the hope of life.

On the other side of the coin, I've talked with many who have experienced an abortion and they tell me these abortion facilities seemed cold and uninviting. Several complained of a lack of privacy.

Their concerns over this lack of privacy struck a chord with me, so recently I checked the web site of a well-known abortion facility, complete with photos of the waiting room. I counted 34 chairs in a room that is just ten feet wide and twenty feet long. Is this incredibly crowded?

Design firms tell us that a physician's waiting room needs about 18 square feet per chair. At this particular abortion center, clients have less than six square feet. It's no wonder abortion clients feel disconnected; as if they are nothing more than the next number in the appointment book.

If our Wall is to be completed, we need to give pregnancy help centers space, and lots of it. Many have the room they need; others are praying for more. These centers also need top-line furniture, and the touch of professional interior decorators. In addition, these centers must have inviting exteriors that tell those outside, "You'll find comfort and hope inside." What if every PHC in our country had the first-class facilities today's client would expect from a top-flight medical provider? If we did, the Planned Parenthoods--the Sanballats, Tobiahs and Geshems--could never match us.

What if PHC locations were so inviting and comfortable, every client could actually sense her burden slipping away the moment she entered the lobby? A pregnancy help center must be a place where anyone, after only a few minutes in the lobby, is able to say, "I can trust these people."

For someone who is facing perhaps the most challenging moment in her life, this first impression could literally make a life-saving difference. These PHCs cannot settle for second-hand furniture, cheap carpets or an office in a worn-out location no other business would want. These centers must be located in prime locations and furnished professionally.

When we make our gates—our facilities—a part of our wall-building mission, the abortion industry will be left behind for a simple reason: Regardless of what the abortion industry *says,* the fact is that they do not have an overriding concern for those who come in the door. No matter how much money they have, they rarely spend it on the needs of the client who wants their services. Instead their funds go toward large salaries for upper level management, sales bonuses (yes, really) and an area we will soon discuss, marketing.

Let's make sure our facilities—our gates—stand apart and above anything the abortion industry can offer. When we complete this portion of our Wall of Hope, we will be one step closer to winning the hearts of a generation that needs us now more than ever.

-The Wall-

Chapter 11
Staffing and Services at the PHC:
The Brick and Mortar of Our Wall of Hope

And it came about, when all our enemies heard of it, and all the nations surrounding us saw it, they lost their confidence; for they recognized that this had been accomplished with the help of God.
—Nehemiah 6:16

Nehemiah's wall was tall, fortified, and thus, impenetrable. The timber, bricks and mortar provided everything needed so that all of the citizens inside those walls would know, without doubt, that they were safe from harm. And as pointed out in the verse above, this strong wall discouraged the enemies of Israel as well.

Pregnancy help centers want their clients to have this same sense of safety, and this is provided through the staff of the PHC. Walk inside a pregnancy help center and you'll find committed paid and volunteer staff members who are dedicated to excellence. Even better, these servants perform their mission out of a love for God and a desire to reflect His image.

When nervous or confused young women and men enter a pregnancy help center, they will find compassion, empathy, and hope.

It's no wonder that when I read exit surveys from those served by PHCs, I see phrases such as . . .

They took the time to listen to me.

I felt comfortable as soon as we started talking.

She cried with me. And asked if she could pray for me. I've never had anyone do that for me before.

I was so scared. But after we talked, I knew everything was going to be okay.

Those serving in PHCs are, at least in their minds, ordinary. As a result, pregnancy help centers are places where humility is genuine, transparency is embraced and where all pull together with a common desire to comfort, to encourage and to provide hope for those who come in the door.

Those who are willing to love make all the difference in the world and that is exactly what we find inside these centers.

In contrast, the abortion industry gives us case after case of abortion practitioners who abuse clients, care nothing about safety and cleanliness, and who treat their own staff members as second-class citizens. The story of Dr. Kermit Gosnell in Philadelphia, who was convicted in 2013 of the deaths of infants born alive after his botched abortions, is only the tip of the iceberg.

The abortion industry of course, attempts to create a perception of being caring, even as evidence against this false narrative grows. So while we watch as abortion providers are shut down for heinous practices and even hauled off to jail, Planned Parenthood and others proudly assert that they offer the best in services for those facing unplanned pregnancies.

We can complain about perceptions if we want. But our most effective response is not to spend our time on what is wrong, but is instead to change these perceptions by strengthening those people inside PHCs, and by offering more and better services. As a result, we will turn the tables.

What if we shifted this entire dynamic so that PHCs, *not* abortion centers, became the place where young people turned for answers? It's not out of the realm of possibility. Not at all.

First, we've noted that as more pregnancy help centers offer ultrasound, women and men who see their children on the screen for the first time are exponentially more likely to choose life for their children. What if every pregnancy help center in America could offer ultrasound to its clients? What if these centers never lacked for nurses and ultrasound technicians because funding was no longer an issue?

Second, we've pointed out that while those favoring abortion tell us that this is "a woman's choice," the fact is that much of the time, the father's point of view has a major impact on the mother's ultimate decision. When dad is excited and supportive of her carrying the baby to term, mom is incredibly more interested in choosing life.

With this in mind, what if every PHC had men on staff to reach out and mentor the men who come inside its doors? Do we think that might make a difference? You're darned right it would. Lives would be saved by the thousands.

What would happen if every PHC had professionals in place to meet the vast array of needs clients face? What if clients were coming to pregnancy help centers with their health issues instead of running to the Planned Parenthoods across the country? What if many of these clients, with facts in hand, chose to make a new decision and wait until marriage? The unplanned pregnancy rate would drop precipitously. As a matter of course, the abortion rate would plummet too.

So, what if we could match the abortion industry in funding for staffing and services, dollar for dollar? Or, what if we could actually *surpass* the abortion industry in each of these areas? We can.

Here are a couple of more truths, from my perspective:

First, when we build our Wall of Hope, prospective clients will be much more likely to choose PHCs over the abortion industry.

Second, if you believe this is a pipe dream and the price tag is unfathomable, stay with me. We're about to see that this is not only manageable, but *much easier* than we might believe.

Let's give these pregnancy help centers the funding to be fully-staffed, with the tools they need to provide the best in care. No one should have to take a pay cut to work at a PHC, and no client should ever be turned away because these centers are short-staffed.

We can do this. And once our Gates are in place and our Wall reaches full-height, we will reach out through our Towers . . .

Chapter 12
Marketing the Pregnancy Help Center: The Towers of Our Wall of Hope

After him the Tekoites repaired another section in front of the great projecting tower and as far as the wall of Ophel.
—Nehemiah 3:27

The towers of Nehemiah's wall were likely striking in height and while they were a home for lookouts to watch for invaders, the towers had another purpose: Those needing the shelter of the wall could see the towers from a distance and knew exactly where to go for hope.

For pregnancy help centers, marketing initiatives create the Tower of the Wall of Hope. From these towers, PHCs call out to those seeking safety, offering refuge from the storm. Those needing these centers must know where they can find true options and true compassion. Without a doubt then, PHCs need the resources not only to advertise their message, but to effectively saturate the markets they serve.

Once we give our PHCs these resources, the abortion industry is going to have a big problem. Because while the Planned Parenthoods spend millions on lobbyists, public relations experts and more, the abortion industry can never communicate a message of hope. Never. Pregnancy help centers can, and will.

This is Nehemiah's story, again. The Sanballats and Tobiahs had a louder megaphone for their message of discouragement and defeat. But it was Nehemiah's message, one of promise; that ultimately resonated with the people.

The challenge for PHCs is that many do not yet have the resources to bring in the experts and focus groups to determine how to best communicate their message. In addition, finding the resources to fully blanket the community with this message is also an obstacle; one which we are about to overcome.

Today, I can tell you: In my work with more than one thousand pregnancy help centers I can confidently say that *not one* CEO has told me that he or she has a fully-funded marketing budget. **Not one.**

Let's change this. When we do, in short order PHCs will be the *first* choice for women and couples facing unplanned pregnancies. When PHCs are the first choice, we know the likelihood that potential clients will seek a second option is much, much lower.

An aside here: abortion centers sell one product; abortion, and yet claim the word, "choice." Nothing could be further from the truth. It is time for those of us who believe in life to reclaim this word, because it is ours.

Pregnancy help centers *are* the home of choice, true choice. At these centers a client is offered many options such as single-parenting, adoption, co-parenting, and marriage. And yes, she is even given the true facts regarding abortion; something abortion centers do not offer. When a PHC does its job, a client walks away knowing all of her (or their) options and can make an informed choice.

To highlight this discrepancy between pregnancy help centers and abortion centers, I was at a PHC in the Midwest while writing this book. One of their clients had visited the local Planned Parenthood office, where she told her counselor she was pregnant and wanted to give life to her child. Do you want to know the advice the Planned Parenthood counselor gave her? *Call the pregnancy help center.*

Let's get this straight: a young lady with a *planned* pregnancy was told by *Planned Parenthood* that because she had chosen life, she needed to go elsewhere. How's that for choice?

When we build the Wall of Hope, the word *choice* will be ours, again. As it should be.

What would happen if a lack of resources no longer hindered these marketing initiatives? What if PHCs were no longer a "best kept secret," but were communicating their message on our television screens, billboards, signage and more? What if potential clients could find information about a local PHC not only on the internet, but also on the radio and even before viewing a popular movie on the big screen?

The PHC message needs to be clear and consistent; honest and forthright. And it will be. The PHC message of help and hope will, in time, overwhelm those who seek to take lives and exploit those facing crisis pregnancy situations.

Nehemiah's message won the day because of its clarity and consistency. The message of PHCs will win, too. Together, we can make sure their Towers are tall, strong, and fortified.

-The Wall-

Chapter 13
The Gates, the Wall and the Towers:
And a Dramatic Shift Toward Life

And I also applied myself to the work on this wall; . . . and all my
servants were gathered there for the work.
--Nehemiah 5:16

Together, we can do this. We can create Gates of excellence. We can build the Wall of staffing and services. And we can raise Towers that send forth a message of truth and hope.

We're on our way to making this happen. Some PHCs have finished the job when it comes to staffing and services. Others have first-rate medical offices that combine professionalism and incredible warmth. Some have accomplished both. A few can even tell us of effective marketing initiatives either in the works or on the drawing table.

But no PHC, not yet anyway, can say all three aspects of the Wall are completed. But that day is coming; you and I are ready to finish the job.

Let me ask you the question I asked myself before writing this book. If we had a manageable plan to build each of these aspects of our Wall of Hope . . . in almost every pregnancy help center in America . . . would you embrace the idea?

Think about it: For forty years we've done so much. And even though we are not yet where we want to be, we've made headway. Finally, the abortion rate is beginning to drop. Still, it is easy for us to find ourselves saying, "Abortion will always be with us."

Yet America's PHCs, if given some help, can compete head-to-head with, and eventually overwhelm, abortion itself. The foundation is in place, waiting for that powerful infusion of resources to create a tipping point that will literally turn our culture upside-down.

Here are a few "What ifs" for us all:

What if each of us truly believed this is possible?

What if we left behind any discouragement, any doubt and any reservation; and committed ourselves to making these centers the first choice?

What if, regardless of the obstacles in our way, we took on the determination of Nehemiah and purposed in our hearts to fulfill this calling?

If we choose this path, we could look back in a few years and know that God used us to save the lives of more than 1 million children every year, creating a culture of life that will endure for the generations to follow. And we will accomplish this mission regardless of election results or court decisions, and without benefit of one government dollar.

I think that's an accomplishment we will consider to be of eternal value.

So the question is, do we believe? The belief we are talking about is a practical one. This isn't about wishing and hoping; it is about each of us taking two manageable steps.

If each of us takes these two steps, we could infuse America's pregnancy help centers with an additional $1 Billion each year. That's "B"--illion. With that additional $1 billion in annual revenue, not one PHC in America would be lacking in resources to accomplish every mission God places in front of it, including the big one: Cutting our abortion rate by 75% or more and saving millions of lives in the next decade.

Here is the fascinating part: None of us will be forced to make a major sacrifice. We don't need to drain our savings, sell all of our worldly goods or begin selling items door-to-door. But if those of us who call ourselves "pro-life" simply participate in a fashion that fits our current circumstances, we have all the resources we need and then some.

Even better, we don't have to create a new organization; we simply need to support those already in place. And while God may call some of us to take on major roles both financially and person-ally, we will likely be surprised at how simple this is.

-The Wall-

Chapter 14
Together We Build

I told them how the hand of my God had been favorable to me and also about the king's words which he had spoken to me. Then they said, "Let us arise and build." So they put their hands to the good work.
—Nehemiah 2:18

Is it actually possible to take the Wall of Hope created by America's PHCs from "half its height" to "complete?" Can we infuse these organizations with all of the resources they need to accomplish the task in front of them? You'd better believe we can.

This is our Wall of Hope Challenge of the 21st century, and like Nehemiah, we're going to get it done.

When we answer this calling and succeed, the results will be easy for all to see.

Setting the stage . . .

To get a clearer picture of what this Wall of Hope can do, let's start with where we stand at the moment. Surveys tell us the average PHC budget is about $230,000. With 2500 pregnancy help centers in this country, this means that right now, we are funding these centers with around $575 million per year.

Based on some data I've gathered from centers around the country, the average PHC donor, whether an individual or a couple, gives roughly $350 each year. This includes everyone from the person who writes a $25 check once a year to the philanthropist who donates $100,000 or more from a stock portfolio.

This $350 figure shows an incredible commitment from many people; at least 1.6 million are already building the Wall of Hope. And we are about to see that if others join this multitude of 1.6 million on the Wall, we can add another $1 billion more quickly than we might think.

With a starting point of $575 million, an additional $1 billion would create an immediate and dramatic impact. Among the 2500 Pregnancy help centers, another $1 billion in funding will mean an *average* of $400,000 in increased resources per center. Larger centers in more populated areas and those with multiple locations will likely gain more funding, while those with budgets of $200,000 or less will still see their donations double or triple.

If PHCs each added somewhere between $200,000 and $600,000 in new funding each year, we would see an amazing transformation in these centers . . .

• PHCs would offer services that match or surpass any abortion-advocacy organization or center

• Every PHC would reach potential clients with a clear, consistent advertising message

• Each PHC would be housed in first-class facilities, offering the perfect environment for life-affirming decisions

• Any new initiative could be fully-funded on Day 1

• Never would a staff member have to leave for financial reasons, because these centers could afford to pay every employee a competitive salary

• Money would never be an issue for PHCs seeking the best and the brightest when they expand their staffs

And this is just the beginning.

Friends, if we pump this kind of funding into our PHCs, groups like Planned Parenthood, even with its current budget of $1 Billion, could never match what these centers offer. These PHCs, and I've spent enough time in them to know, spend their funds so much more wisely it isn't even close. Planned Parenthood is forced to spend a large portion of its income on political and public relations activities, just to keep the government funding rolling in. PHCs don't spend money lobbying for government largesse; they are focused on building the Wall of Hope.

In addition, while PHCs look to pay competitive salaries, they have no interest in rivaling Planned Parenthood, where the top eight executives each earned an average salary of more than $260,000 in 2010. Not only this, CEOs at individual Planned Parenthood affiliates earn an average salary of $158,797.

Those who staff pregnancy help centers aren't in it for the money; they never were. For them, this is a labor of love; a calling from God to reach out to those in need of His love and mercy. That's why at PHCs, I've seen executive directors and others taking pay cuts, placing the needs of clients ahead of their own. We're not going to find this at Planned Parenthood.

Sometimes however, those who serve at PHCs have to leave the calling they love because they cannot afford to stay. Like anyone else, PHC staff members have to pay the bills. When their salaries fall short for too long, there is no other choice. When you and I take our places on the Wall, this will never happen again. Not on our watch.

When we build our Wall of Hope, pregnancy help centers will never again lose a staff member over the subject of dollars, nor will these centers fret over trying to offer competitive salaries when an opening occurs.

PHCs make every dollar count. Give these centers an average of $400,000 in new funding each year and God can use this bunch to not only save hundreds of thousands of lives annually, but to build a new culture of vibrant, faith-focused families as well.

If this is so simple . . .

Someone might well ask, "If this is so easy, why didn't we do this earlier?"

A straight and honest answer, from one who has watched this Wall quietly rise over the past 20 years, is that we were not yet ready. Twenty years ago, I'm not sure if more funding would have been the answer. First, most of today's centers were not yet open. In addition, we noted earlier those PHCs in existence could not yet effectively offer such services as ultrasound. Few had any medical services at all.

Even ten years ago, most PHCs were still learning about the power of offering medical services. In addition, initiatives to reach fathers were just getting started.

Five years ago? These centers were close, but still growing on many fronts. Hundreds of PHCs were still in the formative stages of development.

Today however, the Wall of Hope is rising at a rapid pace. Even the newest of PHCs can quickly pick up on the learning curve from dozens of centers around them. Centers are joining together in partnerships like never before. Fatherhood initiatives abound. Medical services are growing exponentially, mentoring programs are stronger than ever and the stories clients are telling their friends are resonating across cultural and social lines.

As an example of this rapid growth, I was in a Southern college town recently where a group was in the process of opening a PHC. The start-up team for this center knew that a nearby campus of 20,000 college students needed their center to be a fully-functioning medical clinic on day one, not in the far-off future. At their first fundraising dinner, those in attendance caught the urgency of their vision and committed $191,000 toward its opening. In the space of twelve months, this center will go from a dream to reality. That's how fast this Wall is coming together.

So can we accomplish the mission? Absolutely. And the time is now.

-The Wall-

Chapter 15
The Wall of Hope: Our Challenge

When I saw their fear, I rose and spoke to the nobles, the officials and the
rest of the people: "Do not be afraid of them; remember the Lord who is
great and awesome, and fight for your brothers, your sons, your daughters, your
wives and your houses."
—Nehemiah 4:14

Our mission is clear, simple and succinct:

Together, we will bond together to build this Wall of Hope. We will each commit to supporting these centers and the result will be *at least* $1 Billion in new annual funding for America's pregnancy help centers.

When we accomplish this, we can expect to overwhelm those entities that now prey on our young people and their children. The result? We could see our country's abortion rate drop by 75% . . . or more.

So how do we band together to add $1 billion in funding for these centers? In real numbers, let's consider:

The latest census (2010) gave the United States a population of 308 million people. This number, according to census figures, translates into 117 million households.

Let's take those 117 million households and ask, "How many believe in the sanctity of life?" To find our answer, let's look at two recent polls.

A May 2012 Gallup poll told us 50% of Americans consider

themselves pro-life. In November 2012, a Rasmussen poll indicated 38% of Americans hold a pro-life view. The average of these two polls is 44%; meaning that some 50 million households believe in the sanctity of life. Of course, some households are split on these views, but overall, 50 million is a reasonable number for our starting point.

Stay with me here, because we don't need all 50 million of these households to suddenly start pouring thousands of dollars into their local PHCs and PHC-related organizations.

In fact, let's say that only *one in five* pro-life households chose to accept our challenge to build the Wall of Hope. In other words, of every five households that might hold a pro-life view, four might not participate for a variety of reasons, such as lack of information, failing to understand the powerful impact of these centers, or perhaps because of apathy. After all, anyone can answer a poll question but not everyone will act on that set of beliefs.

Yet even if we cut down our participation list by a whopping 80%, we *still* have 10 million families or individual households that are pro-life and likely driven by their faith in God and a desire to protect these young moms, dads and their children. Friends, 10 million families is more than enough to complete our mission. Let's do the math.

What if 10 million families . . .

Gave an average of just **$8.34 per month** in new funding toward America's Wall of Hope, our pregnancy help centers? This is little more than one fast-food meal, probably less than we might pay for a monthly texting plan on our phone and certainly less than a few gallons of gasoline. That's less than $100 per year, barely above a quarter per day.

This isn't to say we should give up any of these items. It is to say however, that $8.34 does not have to mean a major alteration in our monthly budgets.

Guess what? This $8.34, multiplied by 10 million families or individuals, adds up to $83.3 million every single month. And over 12 months, this small commitment of less than $10 each month adds up to . . . **One Billion Dollars.**

The good news

In the previous chapter we noted that $575 million is already flowing into PHCs across the country, and the average contributor gives about $350 per year. And we pointed out that somewhere around 1.6 million individuals and families are already building the Wall of Hope. These people are laying the foundation, waiting for others to join them.

I'm sure many of those 1.6 million individuals and families already on the Wall would give more if asked. But we can add another $1 billion for PHCs each year if another 8.4 million builders stepped up on the Wall.

The better news here is that you and I both know we don't need anywhere close to 10 million families to complete our Wall, because many, many of us will go beyond $8.34 per month. That number is only shown to help us see how simple this really is. There are some reading this book who can give thousands of dollars each year (perhaps hundreds of thousands) to pregnancy help centers and their affiliate organizations.

There are also many of us who can give $50, $75 or $100 each month. Even $15 each month is nearly *double* what we need to complete the task of building our Wall of Hope. And certainly, some of us are struggling financially right now and we're wondering if we can make a difference. If so, remember that *every* contribution to the Wall of Hope, whether in the hundreds of thousands, in the hundreds, or $8.34 each month, brings us closer to a completed Wall.

Raising our Wall of Hope to full height is within our reach. As people of faith it is now incumbent upon us to believe. For 93 years the people of Israel saw a broken-down wall and while they likely had every resource available to rebuild, they chose not to believe. But once Nehemiah convinced them that God was on their side, they could not be stopped.

In fact, our biggest obstacle here is not our checkbooks but our faith. Because once we believe we can do this, there is nothing to hold us back from accomplishing the mission.

If we believe, we will take action.

And if we believe, we will tell others.

Spiritually, we know we have an enemy. This enemy seeks to discourage us, to gradually break our belief in the ability to accomplish the seemingly impossible. He wants us to forget the words of the Book of Hebrews, where we are reminded that "faith is the assurance of things hoped for, the conviction of things not seen (Heb. 11:1)."

The enemy would rather we worry about our resources, fret over those who may oppose our work, or complain about the current state of our nation.

In short, the enemy wants us to do anything *except* **build the wall**.

You and I however, have news for the enemy: we plan to build.

And build we will.

Together, we are about to pour an unprecedented amount of financial support into an enterprise that is already on the rise. In the process, we could very well change the course of history in our country.

Let's get started.

-The Wall-

Chapter 16
We Start With a Clear Picture

So I went up at night and inspected the wall.
—Nehemiah 2:15A

Completing our Wall of Hope is not complicated. Our first step is an easy one: Finding a pregnancy help center close to us.

Locating a nearby PHC is simple enough. We can go online to www.optionline.org and on the home page, type in our zip code or city and state. Within seconds, the address of every PHC within 100 miles of us pops up on the screen. If necessary, we can always expand our search beyond that 100 mile radius.

Then like Nehemiah, we inspect; capturing a clear view of the center's vision, its challenges, and how we can play a role in its future growth.

Most PHCs have web sites to help us gather information. And of course, these centers are only a phone call or an email away if we want to connect with someone who can provide us with more insight.

We can visit these centers as well. Why not set up an appointment for a tour during off-hours to get a first-hand look? Once we find the center that is the perfect match for our gift, we take action. We will write the check, prepare the bank draft, or visit with our accountant or financial planner.

Let's be builders of the Wall of Hope. When we join the challenge of raising $1 Billion in new funding for PHCs, we can be assured that many others are standing on the Wall with us. And those "many others" have stories to tell us as we prepare to join them . . .

Chapter 17
Stories From the Wall of Hope

Come, let us rebuild the wall of Jerusalem . . .
—Nehemiah 2:17B

Our Wall builders are everywhere. They are ordinary people, just like you and me. Some are struggling to make ends meet; others are extraordinarily wealthy. And all of them have stories waiting to be told.

Building the Wall, brick by brick

I opened the envelope and inside was a $25 check. While I realized our center would not rise or fall on that one check I knew there was a family behind this investment with hearts for the work in which we were engaged. If our center were to grow, I realized that hearts just like theirs would be the key. He was a college professor, she a home-schooling mom. They lived in a middle-class home, with a middle class budget. And they were determined to make a difference.

The next month the same couple sent another check, for the same amount.

The gifts continued, month after month. A relationship grew. So did the gifts. Soon they were giving $100. Every month.

As I think about this couple, I realize they and so many like them were the backbone of everything accomplished through our center. Knowing that they would be there every month allowed us to make long-term financial decisions. When a new opportunity or idea presented itself, we knew we could count on monthly supporters like them to see us through to a new future.

If we want to understand just how important these monthly gifts can be, let me ask a question: Would we like to receive a consistent, monthly paycheck that we can count on? Or would we rather our employer say that paychecks might only show up when the company has a few extra dollars? I don't know about you, but I'll take consistency.

It is the same for these centers. Our regular, monthly investments in their success allow the board and staff to make key, long-term decisions regarding new services, more effective outreach and more. A monthly gift of $25, $50 or $100 may not seem exceptional when we look at the overall budget picture, but these gifts are crucial.

What would happen if our entire team of 10 million wall-builders gave an average gift of $25 per month? That's more than *$3 billion per year;* an average of $100,000 *every month* for every PHC in America.

I've visited centers where there are generous supporters giving $100, $300 and even $500 every month. It's not uncommon at all. And I've also seen hundreds of couples and singles who are living paycheck to paycheck and still finding a way to support a ministry with $15, $20 and $35 each month.

Recently I ran across a PHC supporter who lives on a limited, fixed income. She has never given a gift of more than $13 to her local pregnancy help center. But over the years her consistency, every month over the last 17 years, has built up more than $2,000 in gifts that are saving lives, every day. For any of us who says our gifts aren't enough to make a difference, let's sit down and talk to this wonderful woman, who didn't let her financial circumstances stop her from investing in changing lives.

I even met a 16-year-old girl in the South who realized that her local PHC was reaching her peers and supporting her belief in the sanctity of life. With only a part-time, minimum-wage job, she found a way to give $5 every time the monthly calendar turned. When I met her, I realized that there is room on this Wall for every one of us, because *every* gift brings us closer to completing our Wall of Hope.

We can launch our monthly commitment in one of several ways. Commitment cards are available from some centers. Or, we can just jot a note with our first gift, notifying the center of our intentions. Regardless of how we do so, letting the PHC know we would like to make a monthly gift allows the decision makers to be better stewards of funds.

How we give is up to us. We can write a check, give online or even by automatic withdrawals from our bank or credit card accounts. The important point is consistency. It makes all the difference.

One way to build the Wall of Hope? Brick by brick, every month. It is an amazingly effective avenue for accomplishing the mission.

Turning "next" into "now"

At a PHC fundraising dinner in the Southwest, guests responded with gifts and pledges totaling nearly $100,000 to help fund the center for the coming year. Yet during the event, the executive director also pointed to the future, noting that with more clients coming to the PHC, space was an issue. Soon, the center would need a new home.

After the dinner, the executive director received a phone call. "I think I've got the place for you," said the caller. "Let me show it to you. I think you're going to like it."

The building was perfect for the center's needs, but the price was prohibitive. Yet this generous supporter saw he could meet the PHC's need, now. He purchased the building, added another $150,000 for a first-class renovation, top-line furniture and medical equipment; and today the center is thriving like never before.

This is a great example of what can happen when someone sees a way to turn a dream for the future into reality.

No time like the present

As a PHC in the South held a dedication service for a new facility, the executive director mentioned to the small crowd gathered that the center was ready to open its new home, but was still $17,000 short of the funds needed to purchase an ultrasound machine. An offering was taken. While progress toward the $17,000 goal was made, the PHC was still well short of its financial goal.

Afterward however, an elderly couple approached the executive director with tears in their eyes. "Order the machine immediately," the husband said. "God told us to go ahead and pay the balance. The babies can't wait."

The PHC could have opened its new office without the ultrasound machine, certainly. Yet this couple knew that *with* ultrasound, more lives would be touched and ultimately, more lives would be saved.

Both of these stories remind me that there are those among us whom God can use to turn a PHC's "next" into now. Virtually every center has a plan for the future on the drawing board, or a particular need that, if met today, would create a bright tomorrow.

Do you like to give toward specific needs? If so, give the executive director a call and ask what might be on the PHC's "Next" list. Is it a piece of furniture that might assist in making a good first impression on clients? Paint for that room that needs something extra? A flat screen TV to better view a baby pictured by ultrasound?

The CEO might tell you of a need for a new laptop or printer, or of new software that could make the office run more smoothly. Or we might find the center needs that ultrasound machine, an important renovation, or the funds to hire a key staff member.

Extra funds? Check on the center's Visionary Budget or find out what is "Next" on the list of needs. If we want to make an impact with a major gift, this could be one of the smartest phone calls we make.

The power of creativity

A recent email from a PHC in the Mountain West reminds me of how simple it is for any of us to give when we put our minds to the task:

One of our supporters is just twelve years old. Her family has supported our center for years, but what is so precious is that this young lady saves her birthday money and other money she receives throughout the year and buys items for our clients.

Her mom will call and ask what is needed and without fail, this young lady will come walking in with the item she bought with her money. The joy on her face is a true testament that her giving is from the heart.

This girl, not yet a teenager, shows us that if we are committed to building the Wall of Hope, we can always find a way to do so.

Taking the power of creativity to an entirely new level, one couple in the Northeast found a fixer-upper house, purchased it, then invited PHC friends and volunteers to help them renovate in order to resell the home. The result? The couple earned $15,000 on their house-flipping project and donated the profit to the PHC.

From our twelve-year-old friend in the Rockies, to a couple with a passion for renovation, there are literally hundreds of ways to build the Wall of Hope with a little ingenuity and a lot of heart.

A step of faith, on wheels

I'll never forget speaking in a church while I was executive director of a PHC, encouraging those in attendance to participate in our Walk for Life. This Walk is a short, two-mile event where walkers find a few friends to sponsor them with all sizes of financial gifts.

As I finished a brief presentation, I walked to the back of the sanctuary where I met an older woman in a wheelchair. She touched my sleeve as I greeted her and told me, "I'm going to have a friend push me during the Walk. I'll be there."

She told her friends, and they jumped to her side with pledges. She raised more than $700 not only that year, but for each of the next several years before her passing. She left an indelible imprint on my life, reminding me that if we have faith, nothing can stop us from supporting the moms, the dads and the children who rely on PHCs for hope.

A kind way to give (A Gift in Kind)

In the midst of renovations, a PHC in the East was hoping to purchase new furniture for its lobby. A couple came forward and asked to help. The couple brought in an interior designer who made suggestions; then they sat down with the executive director and crafted a design plan.

With the plan in place, the couple went out and bought each piece of furniture listed, and all of the accessories necessary to create a first-class environment and impress every client who walks in the door. Theirs is a great example of how a Gift in Kind can provide a PHC with a shot of momentum.

The phrase "Gift in Kind" defines those times when, instead of giving funds, we give actual goods. For many of us, a Gift in Kind can be a tax-wise investment in the center, and simple at the same time.

At one PHC in the South, renovation costs were cut by thousands when the owner of a dry wall company called the CEO and said, "Just tell me what you need. My men and I will be down there and get it done. No charge."

At another, I walked by a conference room located just off of the PHC's lobby, furnished with top of the line seating and a conference table we might see at a Fortune 500 company. How did they pay for this? They didn't. A supporter was making changes at his office and offered the furniture, in pristine condition, to benefit the center.

This gift made a tremendous difference. For one, clients can see the conference room through the glass walls, creating a professional first impression that leads to confidence in the center itself. Second, during off hours the center loans this room to other organizations and businesses; offering all of these groups a positive view of the center and building community goodwill.

Gifts in Kind such as these are a secret weapon for PHCs. The Planned Parenthoods of this world get a lot of financing for their political efforts, but little or no support for their actual services, for good reason. While some society elites and left-leaning foundations love to tout their support for "abortion rights," few want to get caught up in the ugly business of abortion.

As a result, we won't see abortion-friendly, Hollywood A-list celebrities gathering together to paint the exterior of an abortion center or offering to purchase surgical tools for late-term abortions. No, they give their money to abortion-promoting political action committees; then trot off to *save* trees and animals.

On the other hand, our family of faith understands that the success of a Christian organization depends on our support. And we step up in any way we can.

An invitation to the Wall of Hope

Standing in front of an intimate gathering at a PHC banquet in the Mountain West, I was about to make the case for funding the ministry. Before I could get started however, a young man in his 30s made his way toward me with his hand out, silently asking for the microphone.

Handing a microphone to someone not on the program can be a risk. Who knows what might be said? In this situation however, I noticed where the young man had been sitting; at the table of a nationally-known philanthropist whom I had met earlier in the evening. I decided to take my chances and would soon find out he was the man's son.

I smiled and gave him the floor. The young man immediately took control of the room with humor. "Seeing as my father wants to give away my inheritance," he said to laughter, "He would like to match every gift tonight, up to $50,000."

In a room of perhaps 125 people, more than $100,000 was raised for a fledgling PHC. It was an amazing moment, made possible by someone who understood that his leadership gift would serve as in invitation, paving the way for others to join the Wall of Hope.

Many reading this book have the same ability. You see that a major gift of $5,000, $50,000 or even $500,000 can encourage others. Many times, the announcement of a large gift leads to more and more giving. Your gift could launch a campaign, provide the center with new momentum, or give rise to a new vision that will change your community.

Bringing future dreams to reality

Another time I was working with a board in a quiet, Southern town. The doors of the PHC were barely open and its budget was a reasonable $70,000. Yet this PHC was already looking toward a bigger future. And as we talked, the phone rang.

On the other end of the line was a financial advisor, informing the center that a $150,000 gift was on the way. The executive director looked at me in shock; then tears of joy began to slip down her cheeks. Suddenly, the center's vision for the future was right in front of her.

As one center prepared for a multi-million dollar capital campaign, the CEO of a major Christian foundation sat down with the center's executive director and made it plain that the foundation was most interested in funding those endeavors that are "so big that success is impossible without God."

The center's goal, which includes creating an abortion-free community, was certainly big enough. But there was a problem. Unless someone stepped up with a major gift, the center would be constantly working to meet current budgetary needs and would never be able to launch new initiatives and give life to the vision.

The CEO of the Christian foundation saw the obstacle and determined to meet the challenge. Within weeks, the foundation gave $350,000 to kick off the campaign. Soon, others followed with gifts of all sizes. Today, a center with big dreams is well on its way to completing a mission that without God, is impossible.

A final word

To close this section, let's consider an 8-year-old boy I had the joy of meeting as I was writing this book. His name is Dillon, he lives near Tampa, Florida and he is quite the entrepreneur. He operates his own business, *Dillon's Second Chance Golf Balls*, whereby Dillon finds wayward golf balls in the woods and lakes at a course where he lives, and resells them at a discounted price.

Even at this young age, Dillon makes giving to the pregnancy help center near his home a priority. Taking a portion of his profits, in December of 2011 Dillon made a contribution of $32.25 to the center. But he was just getting started.

In December of 2012, Dillon was back to make his yearly gift. This time, his donation was $107.20. Those at the center were stunned. Here was a child in third grade, deciding that saving the lives of those he did not know or could not see took precedence over new video games, Lego projects, a bike, sports gear or anything else we can imagine an elementary student might want.

I was told about Dillon and his story as I was preparing to speak at a fundraising dinner for Dillon's chosen center. All I could think of was, *If an 8-year-old boy can give $107.20, what am I willing to do?*

At the dinner where we introduced Dillon, I asked Dillon's parents if I could bring him up on the stage and let him tell his story.

All of us were captured by the moment. Together, we realized that this evening was not going to be about simply raising a few dollars for a nice cause. No, this night focused on our shared belief that the Wall of Hope could, and would, be built in this community.

In short, our mission was now bigger than any of us in that room. In the end, men and women joined together to give and pledge just over $107,000; three times more than the event had ever raised before and almost exactly 1,000 times the amount of Dillon's gift. How is that for a God-ordained coincidence?

And it all started because of a young boy who traipses through the woods and digs into the lakes to find a few golf balls—so that he can save the lives of children he may never know in this lifetime.

At fundraising events I am usually the person who asks guests to give. As a natural result, I have the privilege of "leading" the giving. Not this time. As I looked at Dillon standing next to me on that stage I saw Isaiah's words in plain view: *And a little boy will lead them* (Isaiah 11:6).

Dillon's story reminds me that all of us, no matter where we are in our economic circumstances, can participate at some level in this mighty endeavor. And when we do, nothing can keep us from accomplishing our mission.

We've considered several ways we can give to our PHC, and believe me, there are more. We could turn this book into an encyclopedia if we considered wills, trusts, and many other gift options.

Most important however, is our hearts.

If our hearts are captured by this vision to truly turn our culture toward life, we will find a way to give.

If our hearts are focused, there is no limit to how far we can go toward completing our Wall of Hope.

And if our hearts are trusting in the God who can do all things, we will accomplish what appears to be impossible: We will create a new culture of life that is an amazing testament to the love of God and His presence in our lives through His son, Jesus Christ.

Chapter 18
Shoulder to Shoulder on the Wall of Hope

Now the sons of Hassenaah built the Fish Gate; they laid its beams and hung its doors with its bolts and bars.

Next to them Meremoth the son of Uriah the son of Hakkoz made repairs. And next to him Meshullam the son of Berechiah the son of Meshezabel made repairs. And next to him Zadok the son of Baana also made repairs.
—Nehemiah 3: 2-3

If we read the third chapter of Nehemiah, we're going to notice a band of committed workers, standing next to each other on the wall as they built. We can do the same today. Once we take our place with those already building the Wall of Hope, our next step is to invite others to stand with us.

Let's go back for a moment and remind ourselves: Because of the foundation already in place, we have a window of opportunity to make PHCs across America **the first choice** of women and couples facing unplanned pregnancies. When PHCs are the first choice, every piece of objective data tells us that the second choice, abortion, will drift toward obscurity.

In addition, when PHCs are the first choice, this momentum will give boost to all other areas of the life-affirming movement, including the political and legal fronts. For instance, when Planned Parenthood comes clamoring for government dollars, a pro-life legislator can point to PHCs and say, "*These* centers are already helping young women and young men and their approach is working. We *don't need* Planned Parenthood anymore."

Pregnancy help centers are getting stronger. A surge in growth now could be a tipping point that will forever shift our nation toward celebrating the joy of life once again.

We need to think about this as well: Great movements of social change almost always begin when groups of people pull together, building from the ground up. These movements take off because while leaders emerge, the true power comes from individuals who catch the vision and involve those around them, causing powerful and exponential growth.

Right now, we simply need more people. There are many individuals and families who carry a pro-life view who, for many reasons, haven't yet thought of supporting a pregnancy help center. If they knew how close we are to completing our Wall of Hope, they would join us.

Spreading the word is not a difficult task. We don't need glitzy ad campaigns, slogans or celebrities. That's the other dynamic of great social movements; ordinary people, not slick marketing, make the difference.

This is where you and I come in, and our next step is not complicated at all. We need to engage a few friends. That's it.

Our friends are in our Sunday school classes, Bible studies and small groups. They are on Facebook, Twitter and other social media. Friends are on our email lists, they come to our homes for dinner and they want to know what is going on in our lives. We have every reason to let them know, because many of our friends believe as we do and would love to be involved. We have the opportunity to tell them how.

You are already reading this book and you see the Wall of Hope Challenge. We are looking for 10 million individuals and families to step forward and commit to financially support at least one pregnancy help center and—or—the state and national organizations that assist these centers (see the Appendix for information on this option).

The Wall of Hope web site (www.wallofhopechallenge.com) provides all of the information needed to communicate this vision to those you know.

It's interesting; I was about to use this paragraph to relate ideas on how to effectively post on Facebook, what to write in an email to a friend, all of that stuff. But if you use these or other communication devices, you don't need me to tell you how to use them. There is no reason for pages of tutorials. All we need are people who are motivated; who see what *can* happen in our country if we finish this project.

By the way, when it comes to Facebook and other social media, let's be clear with our friends: we want them to go beyond *liking* our status. We want them to take action. This is the perfect time for us to see amazing results, and we don't want to miss our moment.

Because if, with a little faith, we realize that our golden opportunity to turn this culture toward life is, to use a Biblical phrase, is "at hand," we will act. We won't be reticent to do our part, we will be *ready*.

No one will have to tell us what to do. In fact, there may be surprising moments when we suddenly think of a new name of someone who could join us on the Wall of Hope. We won't need a proven strategy or method. We will do what we always do with friends, whether it is a quick email, a phone call, Tweet, or a Facebook message.

And, if this short book encourages you as you consider your role on the Wall of Hope, why not purchase copies for friends? We priced *The Wall* modestly so that gifting to friends is affordable, and a portion of the proceeds goes back to pregnancy help centers and their affiliate organizations. Amazon has a "Give as a Gift" button on its site, and if you choose the Kindle version of *The* Wall, any computer can download the free reading Application. The www.wallofhopechallenge.com page has information on easy distribution to friends, too.

Regardless of how we connect with friends, the truth is that we can do this. And though I'm just guessing, we noted earlier that we likely have 1.6 million individuals and families already building the Wall of Hope. We can bring in 8.4 million more friends, and we can do so quickly.

Here is a question worth considering. If someone were to tell us that inviting just three people to join us in this endeavor could literally save one million or more lives each year and create a legacy of life so prevalent that perhaps the very idea of ending a pregnancy would become more and more obsolete, would we get involved?

I'm guessing we would, in a heartbeat.

That's just three people. If we want to go further, we can.

But if we—you and I—step out, many of our friends will stand with us and build. And while I mentioned the possibility in raising $1 billion in new funding for pregnancy help centers, you and I both know that if this and similar ideas catch fire, $1 billion will be just the starting point.

As these funds are raised, you may choose to take a third step, too.

Chapter 19
A Third Step: Rolling up our Sleeves

And the people blessed all the men who volunteered to live in Jerusalem.
—Nehemiah 11:2

Building our Wall of Hope takes funding. But once we make this commitment and begin sharing this idea with our friends, let's keep in mind another effective way we can build: taking our place on the Wall *inside* a pregnancy help center.

PHCs are always looking for staff members, whether paid or volunteer. These centers need everything from experts in their fields to those who say, "Whatever you need, count on me to pitch in."

In one pregnancy help center in the South, a male college student came in with just that approach, asking, "What can I do to help?" He was asked to clean the office and restrooms once a week. Was he willing?

He was, and that's where he got his start as he pursued his degree in social work. Later he would become president of one of the nation's leading adoption agencies.

Another story involves a physician who was a part of a small-group men's Bible study that met in the pre-dawn hours once a week. At one of the meetings, a PHC's executive director mentioned the need for a volunteer physician to lead the center's medical arm. The physician didn't hesitate, offering his services. "You don't need to ask," he said with a smile. "I'll do it." Today that center has one of the PHC movement's leading medical clinics and is often called upon to assist other centers across the country.

As PHCs grow, the need for those experienced in many fields increases . . .

Physicians
Nurses
Lab Technicians
Ultrasonographers
Marketing and Advertising
Web Design
Public Relations/Print Media
Audio/Visual
Attorneys
Accountants
Office Administrators
Counselors
Psychologists
Teachers
Leadership Coaches
Architects
Construction Workers and Contractors
Facilities Maintenance
Landscaping

This list could go on and on. And yet, these centers are also looking for those who are willing to learn, to listen and to contribute in any way needed.

Should we have the opportunity to give our time and talents, the extent of our commitments will vary, of course. Some of us can give as much as several hours each week; others may only have an hour or so each month. Or, we may be called upon to fill a role in a project that comes up only once a year or so.

As with our financial giving, everything is dependent on our hearts. Once our hearts are committed, everything else falls into place.

If possible then, let's also consider offering our gifts of service. Our willingness to lend a hand may lead to thousands and thousands of dollars in savings, and expanded services for the PHC in our area.

A manageable plan

Our mission to build the Wall of Hope is not dependent on an elaborate scheme. Instead, it is simple.

•First, we give at a level that fits our economic circumstances. All of us can find a way to give locally; many of us can go on to give statewide and nationally as well.

•Second, we ask a few others to join us. We can do so in one of the ways we've mentioned, or choose our own avenue.

•Third, many of us can answer the call to step inside the center and offer our time and talents.

One. Two. Three. When we come together with a unified purpose and, as Nehemiah said, "A mind to work," we will complete construction on our 21st century Wall of Hope. And we can be assured that our culture will take note, launching a shift toward honoring the sanctity of life once again.

-The Wall-

Chapter 20
Let's Build a Wall

Now at the dedication of the wall of Jerusalem they sought out the Levites from all their places, to bring them to Jerusalem so that they might celebrate the dedication with gladness, with hymns of thanksgiving and with songs to the accompaniment of cymbals, harps and lyres.
—Nehemiah 12:27

As we consider today's political and social landscape, we as Christians have the choice to respond in one of two ways:

We can choose to view our current circumstances with discouragement, frustration and hopelessness.

We can fret, wondering whether our country will ever return to the values she once cherished.

Or, we can choose to respond as Nehemiah. We can build a Wall of Hope.

By choosing to build, we are capturing this moment as our God-given opportunity to showcase the Body of Christ in action. We have our foundation; 2500 pregnancy help centers standing together, ready for our participation.

If we step up and say, "Now is the time," the bricks are ready to be placed on the Wall. All it takes is our bonding together and saying, "Count me in."

Roe v. Wade and its consequences have been with us for 40 years, an entire generation. The time is now for a *new* generation, a Generation of Life ushered in by the building of the Wall of Hope.

That's *The Wall of Hope Challenge*. It's a Wall of protection for those facing the cultural temptations and battles of today, and for their children waiting to be born; wanting nothing more than to celebrate their first smiles, their first steps, and their first birthdays. Once we get started, once we take our stand on that Wall, there is no limit to what God can do with each of us.

When we step out, God moves

When I was a young executive director of a PHC, our center had the opportunity to purchase the building where we were operating, but we had few funds in our capital account. Due to a series of circumstances beyond our control, we had one week to raise $54,000 for a down payment. If we could raise those funds, renting out other spaces in the building would take care of our mortgage payments.

But we needed $54,000 first.

Our board president encouraged me to create a list of those who could give major gifts, and I came up with twelve names. With list in hand and some fear and trembling, I picked up the phone. One generous friend offered $5,000. So did another. I kept calling.

But in the process of my phone calls, something surprising happened. People who had no idea of our situation began *calling me*. One friend called just to say hello and asked what I was doing. When I told him of our situation he said, "We just received an inheritance and wanted to give $5,000 to a ministry. Would you be interested?" Why yes I was; as a matter of fact.

One of our volunteer staff members dropped by my office and asked if there was anything new happening. When I told her, she went home and told her husband, a good man, but also a man for whom faith in God was not yet important. She attended church; he did not.

That night, he called me. "I don't know what all goes on there," he told me, "But it has been a great influence on my wife. I'd like to give $10,000." And that's exactly what he did. Later, he would change his mind about God, making the decision to follow Jesus Christ. Today, he is an amazing example of what it means to be a Christian.

Another friend called later in the week just to check in. Though he was not on my list, when I mentioned our situation he responded, "Why didn't you call me earlier? My wife and I would like to give $20,000."

In the end, my phone calls reached friends who gave us $16,000. What amazed me however, is that those unexpected calls I received brought in $54,000, for a total of $70,000. We had enough for an even stronger down payment *and* extra funds to help us maintain our new investment.

Before this particular need arose, I had never picked up the phone to ask for a major gift. But I had to step out of my comfort zone and at least try, though to be honest I was afraid we would fall far short of our goal. To me, the moral of this story is that God smiles when we step out with a little faith and attempt something bigger than what we believe we can accomplish.

When we take on the impossible, I believe God rolls up His sleeves, turns to Jesus at His right hand and says with a grin, "Now watch this." In our center's situation, He touched the hearts of many I would have never imagined, more than meeting our need.

The *Wall of Hope Challenge* is bigger than what we can accomplish on our own, certainly. In truth, simply writing this book is a challenge for me, as those thoughts creep in to say, "What if this endeavor fails?" And yet, I believe God is smiling; waiting for us to answer the challenge and take the first steps of faith in this journey.

For some, these first steps involve placing a center in a monthly budget where it is hard to find room. And for those of us in this category, I say this: Just do as God asks. We have no idea what He will do when we step out in faith, offering what we can.

And there are those reading this book—you know who you are—who are saying, "It is time to make a legacy gift." For you, a gift of $100,000, $500,000, or $1 million or more is not out of the question.

Together, we can reach this goal and even beyond. It starts with our commitment.

As I write, I realize that I'm writing this book to many who are *already* supporting these ministries and building the Wall of Hope. I'm there with you. Jennifer and I, with our five children, are considered a regular, middle-class family just trying to pay the bills.

And this year, we have the joy of supporting more than two dozen PHCs with monthly gifts for each. It is an honor to do so. So as I write to all of us who are already giving, I say we ought to consider taking it up one more notch. This may be the time when all of those past gifts, combined with some new ones, finally turn the tables and bring about the dream we've always wanted: A Wall of Hope.

It would not be fair to ask you to do something Jennifer and I will not. So we commit to add to our current giving, just as we are asking you. These new gifts will be our way of joining the challenge. We're choosing to step up. Join us, and let's complete the Wall we've already started.

First then, let's *all* make the commitment to give. From there, God can show each of us both the size of our gifts, and exactly how to make our gifts. In addition, He will show us where our gifts should go. We're on our way to a $1 billion Wall of Hope, a structure that will withstand anything and anyone, and a Wall that will protect all who enter.

In addition, Jennifer and I plan to reach more than 1000 people through several of the methods I've listed in this book. Some will receive this book as a gift; others will get an email from us. And yes, I'll use social media as well. If anyone should be active in reaching our 10 million Wall Builders, your author should be at the front of the line.

Let's remind ourselves again: with God's help, we can do this. When we complete our mission, the Wall of Hope will be at full height, PHCs will be the first choice for all who need us, hundreds of thousands of lives will be saved and more and more joyful families will be welcoming children into their homes. And once again, the culture in the United States will be one that celebrates *life*.

It's time. The challenge is in front of us. Let's build a Wall.

Follow the progress of the Wall of Hope at
www.wallofhopechallenge.com

Purchase copies of *The Wall* for friends at
www.amazon.com

-The Wall-

TOGETHER WE BUILD

Questions for Reflection
(For individuals and small groups)

◆ In Scripture, we see time after time that God works through His people to accomplish more than we can imagine. Reflect on situations in your own life where this has taken place.

◆ As we consider the Wall of Hope, list specific ways we can pray for this endeavor. We can refer to this list regularly as we build together.

♦ The mission of building our Wall of Hope, and lowering our country's abortion rate to pre-1973 levels, is certainly a challenge. Some in the Christian community may see this goal as impossible to achieve. What are some specific things we can say as we respond to those who do not believe we can complete this mission?

♦ The pro-life community is comprised of people from across the economic spectrum, from those battling to make ends meet to the enormously wealthy. Prevailing wisdom might tell us that we should look almost exclusively to those with the greatest resources to fund the Wall of Hope. Why might God's perspective be different? How would a wide range of participants help strengthen our entire endeavor?

♦ When you consider the different giving options outlined in this book, name a few that appeal most to you. What are some other ideas?

♦ When we as the Body of Christ complete our mission of raising at least $1 billion each year in new funding for PHCs across the country, we will see our country's abortion rate drop drastically. And yet because of the faith outreach of these centers, what other positive results might we see in our churches and in our communities?

-The Wall-

I CHOOSE TO BUILD: AN ACTION PLAN
(For individuals and small groups)

First, I pray . . .
What are some specific ways we can pray for our local PHCs and for national and statewide affiliate organizations?

As we participate in the Wall of Hope, how can we pray for our country and its receptiveness to our message?

What are some concrete ways we can pray for and encourage each other as we take action?

Preparing to take action

First, to locate our local PHC:

www.optionline.org or Yellow Pages

Once we locate our nearest center, find its web site for more information, or call for a donor packet.

To find our statewide network, if one is available:

www.heartbeatservices.org/connections/coalitions

Or call my local PHC to find out more.

To find a national network or organization to support:

See **Appendix**, listing several national organizations leading the PHC movement.

My Personal Journey Begins Here

Many times, the greatest accomplishments begin with simple actions. In *The Wall*, we outlined three steps that could, should we choose to take them, save hundreds of thousands of lives and turn our country back toward life once again.

Just like with Nehemiah and his wall, success depends on our choice to participate, and on our choice to involve others.

Below are the two steps we can personally take to build our Wall of Hope. Join the hundreds of thousands of us already on the Wall by making these two choices a part of your life journey. Soon, we may find that we've been used by God to create a new culture . . . of *life*.

The first step: I give

After making my decision regarding how I will give and where my first donation will go, on this date I joined the Wall of Hope with a financial gift:

_____

The second step: I invite others

Who are friends who would likely be interested in this endeavor?

_____

_____

_____

_____

I have now connected with at least three friends by this date:

_____

And Now . . .

Connect with the community of faith as we build the Wall of Hope together:

www.wallofhopechallenge.com

Here you'll find stories on how this Wall is rising throughout the country and encouragement as we grow. Just like Nehemiah, we are about to accomplish a mission just waiting for us as we step forward in faith.

Appendix
Building Statewide, and Nationally, too

When we consider our giving, let's keep in mind those national organizations that are often the first resource a PHC turns to for training, expert counsel and support. Without these, PHCs would be constantly re-inventing the wheel, not knowing what works and what does not.

In addition, a powerful idea created in one PHC can be brought to a national organization and disseminated to all within days.

These affiliate networks bring PHCs together as a unified force, and assist PHCs in maintaining excellence in standards of care. In essence, these national organizations are the mortar in the Wall of Hope. Because of this, our gifts often multiply across the country when given to national networks such as Heartbeat International, CareNet, The National Institute of Family and Life Advocates, Focus on the Family's Option Ultrasound initiative, and more.

What would happen if each of us added one of the following organizations to our giving? With millions of dollars in new funding, these affiliate networks could multiply their national impact, raising the profile of PHCs and bringing these local centers a major step closer to becoming the first choice for every woman or couple facing an unplanned pregnancy. Listed on the following pages are a few of these organizations:

-The Wall-

Heartbeat International
Mission:
"Heartbeat International works to inspire and equip Christian communities worldwide to rescue women and couples from abortion through the development of neighborhood pregnancy help centers, maternity homes, and adoption services."
www.heartbeatinternational.org
Columbus, OH

CareNet
Mission:
"Care Net is a Christ-centered ministry whose mission is to promote a culture of life within our society in order to serve people facing unplanned pregnancies and related sexual issues."
www.care-net.org
Lansdowne, VA

-The Wall-

The National Institute of Family and Life Advocates (NIFLA)
Mission:
"Provide pregnancy resource centers with legal resources and counsel with the aim of developing a network of life-affirming ministries in every community across the nation in order to achieve an abortion-free America."
www.nifla.org
Fredericksburg, VA

Focus on the Family
Focus on the Family provides key resources for PHCs around the country and is also home for "Option Ultrasound," an initiative helping to provide ultrasound services for PHCs.
www.focusonthefamily.com
Colorado Springs, CO

We can also give to a statewide network of pregnancy help centers. While we can't list all of the statewide networks in this book, any of us can check in with our local PHC and ask if there is a statewide organization we can support, along with our local center. In addition, we can visit the following web site for more information on statewide and regional networks:

www.heartbeatservices.org/connections/coalitions

-The Wall-

About the author

Kirk Walden has more than 30 years of experience in the pro-life arena, from political campaigns and public policy to his current work with hundreds of crisis pregnancy ministries across the United States.

After serving nine years as executive director of a crisis pregnancy center, in 2000 Kirk founded LifeTrends, a company that assists these centers in the areas of development, communication and vision-casting. Today LifeTrends' flagship publication, *The LifeTrends Connection*, reaches more than 2000 pregnancy help centers and ministries in the U.S. and around the world.

In addition, Kirk shares his passion for life with audiences across the country. Through LifeTrends and his keynote presentations at fundraising events, Kirk has played a major role in raising more than $25 million for America's pregnancy help centers in the last decade.

He and his wife Jennifer have five children and live near Nashville, Tennessee.

To invite Kirk to speak at your church or event, contact Ambassador Speakers Bureau:

www.ambassadorspeakers.com
(615) 370-4700

-The Wall-